STRANGERS IN A STOLEN LAND:

American Indians in San Diego 1850-1880

Richard L. Carrico

Sierra Oaks Publishing Co.
1987

Library of Congress Cataloging-in-Publication Data

Carrico, Richard L.
  Strangers in a Stolen Land.

1. San Diego Indians–History. 2. Indians of North America–California–
History. 3. Indians of North America–California–Governmental Relations.
I. Carrico, Richard L. II. Title. III. Title: American Indians in San Diego,
1850-1880.

Preassigned Library of Congress Catalog Card number 86-063076

ISBN 0-940113-03-1

This book was originally published by San Diego State University Publications in American Indian Studies and is reprinted with the permission of
the editor.

Dedicated to Paul and Greta Ezell

Table of Contents

Preface vii

Chapter I
Introduction 1

Chapter II
Before the Strangers:
A Prehistoric Overview 5

Chapter III
Mission and Rancho:
Sowing Seeds of Destruction 13

Chapter IV
Local Relations:
Native Americans in American San Diego 18

Chapter V
Separate and Unequal:
Legalizing The Dispossession 37

Chapter VI
Suffering for the Great Cause:
Years of Neglect, 1850-1865 45

Chapter VII
Toward a Reservation System 1865-1874 60

Chapter VIII
Compression and Containment:
Adoption of a Reservation System, 1874-1880 75

Chapter IX
And Still They Endure 89

Footnotes 95

Bibliography 115

Index 125

PREFACE

The history of American Indians living in San Diego County has virtually been ignored by historians. The reasons are clear. As many residents in the county have shunned the Indians, so have historians. San Diego's Indians did not fit the popular image of "great" Indians. They did not ride about on horseback, raiding wagon trains and frontier forts. They did not adorn themselves in fluttering feathers, colorful beads, and buckskin breachcloths. San Diego Indians did not chase across the lands, hunting bison and living in tipis. Instead, the Indians of San Diego were industrious people who hunted, gathered, fished, and farmed on a limited basis. Their history is not filled with glorious victory, nor is it one only of destruction and death. Influenced by Spain since 1769, the Indians of San Diego were forced to cope with the institutions of Spanish settlement. Missions, presidios, and pueblos significantly influenced the Indians of California, including those who lived in what is today San Diego County.

The settlement of Hispanics on lands once considered the sole domain of American Indians in San Diego brought about the destruction of native peoples. In addition to being forced to accept Spanish laws, religion, and economic development, the Indians suffered severely from European diseases, such as smallpox, chickenpox, measles, mumps, influenza, and the common cold. Without the natural biological immunities carried by Euro-Americans, the diseases ravaged the Indians, destroying entire bands. The epidemics that swept across California were worse than the Black Death known to Europeans during the Middle Ages. The Indians could do little to battle the diseases, except move away from the Spanish settlements, churches, and forts, thereby spreading the diseases further. Some Indians moved while others remained, living within the towns built by Spaniards, particularly the town of San Diego.

In 1846 the United States invaded California, claiming the land by right of conquest and then by treaty. With the American invasion of California came the establishment of American law and government, including those laws associated with Indian affairs and those governmental bodies skilled in handling American Indian policy. Overnight, the United States forced the Indians of San Diego to contend with new laws and policies created by a government far removed from the Pacific Coast. Indians continued their association with Hispanic citizens of the region, while at the same time, they learned to cope with the new Anglo citizenry. Hispanics and Anglos shared a common feeling toward Indians and Indian rights. The Indians of San Diego suffered politically, economically, and legally as a result.

The noted historian Alfred North Whitehead felt that ideas were not static, he saw them as active elements of life and thought. To paraphrase Whitehead, merely having ideas is not sufficient action, something must be done about them. They are to be acted upon, used, and revised to form still more ideas. The ideas that form the basis of this book were born as a thesis topic more than a decade ago, grew to a series of published articles, then went into dormancy and have bloomed again with grafts of new thoughts fertilized by the rich loam that other scholars provided.

As one might expect, more than ten years of nuturing and cross fertilization with scholars, students, American Indians, and the lay public accumulates a large body of debts and gratitude to be expressed. I gratefully acknowledge the initial encouragement of David Weber of Southern Methodist University to undertake research on Indian life in San Diego and for demanding professionalism in both research and scholarship. David planted the seeds and Cliff Trafzer of San Diego State University brought the project into fruition with his suggestion to publish the book and by serving tirelessly as editor. I owe personal and intellectual debts to Dr. Paul H. Ezell who first sparked my interest in California Indians. Fortunately for me, even after his retirement from teaching, Paul was always somewhere close at hand inquiring, "How is the work going?" often at times when, in fact, it was not going at all.

Two valued friends, George Phillips and Jeanne Munoz commented on, and critiqued, earlier versions of this work and greatly assisted me in broadening the perspective. The editors and publishers of the **Journal of California and Great Basin Anthropology**, the **Journal of San Diego History**, the **Westerner's Brand Book**, and the **Western States Jewish Historical Society Quarterly** are thanked for publishing several earlier chapters of this work and for graciously allowing me to reprint modified versions of those publications in this book.

The staffs of several libraries and archives are gratefully acknowledged for their efforts. Rhoda Kruse, archivist for the San Diego Public Library California Room deserves special mention as do the desk staffs at the Hubert H. Bancroft Library at Berkeley; the Henry Huntington Library; the Los Angeles Public Library; the Government Documents Department at San

Diego State University's Malcolm Love Library; and the San Diego Historical Society Archives.

Expressions of thanks would not be complete without acknowledging several California Indians. Locally Fern Southcutt, Vince Ibanez, Henry Rodriguez, and Tom Lucas helped me understand the beauty and complexity of their history. To the north my Chumash friends from the United Chumash Council and Santa Ynez Indian Reservation have provided stimulation and increased my awareness of their rich heritage. Their struggle for identity is a mirror reflecting a history of European domination and misunderstanding that continues in our time.

To my co-workers, colleagues, and management at WESTEC Services, Inc., all I can say is thanks for your patience and understanding. Individually and as a corporation, WESTEC has supported this project and allowed me uncommon latitudes.

Susan Carrico, my wife and friend, deserves more thanks than I can ever express. Lastly, there is my mother, to whom I am ever grateful for transplanting us from Indiana to California, otherwise this might well have been the story of the Kickapoo instead of the Kumeyaay and their neighbors.

San Diego, California   Richard L. Carrico

OLD ROSARIA
of Pala Reservation, 1904.
Courtesy San Diego Historical Society

Chapter I

Introduction

These were tumultuous years, the three decades from 1850-1880, and America appeared ready to burst at its ever-expanding seams. In terms of Euro-American history, these thirty years saw a parade of eight presidents from the sublime, Millard Fillmore and Franklin Pierce, to the well known, Abraham Lincoln and Ulysess S. Grant. America's non-Indian population rocketed from slightly more than 23 million in 1850 to over 50 million in 1880 while whole Indian tribes vanished from the land of their ancestors. Cattle trails, iron rails, and rutted wagon roads replaced Indian paths that once branched across the land. A bloody civil war was fought, a second-rate actor gunned down a troubled president, and a flamboyant brevet general gained mythological status at Little Big Horn.

Throughout all of this, American Indian history weaves a continuous thread. It is a moving panorama as Cherokee leaders Stand Watie and John Ross fought on opposite sides in the War of the States, Little Wolf pleaded with Abraham Lincoln for peace, Black Kettle flew the Stars and Stripes amidst Chivington's murderous onslaught at Sand Creek, and Sitting Bull directed the force of native power against George Armstrong Custer. Indians performed disparate, and indeed desperate, action, all with a common goal: to find a place where the white man and his sickness would not come, a place where horse soldiers were forbidden, and bullets would not spit down on Indian families.

The larger play, that of national history from 1850 to 1880, reflected and echoed throughout southern California. As federal Indian policy metamorphosed from the do-nothing stance of President Millard Fillmore to the humanistic, but unfulfilled plans of President Lincoln and beyond to Grant's Peace Policy, the thousands of San Diego Native Americans endured and persisted. The tribes, or more correctly, tribelets, are far less familiar to Americans than those on center stage of United States history. The Luiseno, Cupeno, Cahuilla, Ipai, and Tipai were not then, and are not now, household words. In an almost perverse measure of notoriety and fame, no American trucks, automobiles, or recreation vehicles carry these Indian names. They have yet to be discovered by the Image Makers.

At a time when Americans are taking a serious look at the ethnic diversity that characterizes the United States, new knowledge and insight has encouraged better appreciation of history and contributions of minorities. As the once sole occupant of the entire continent, the story of the American Indian from time of initial European contact to current events is a history of its own making and telling, influenced by, but uniquely separate from Euro-American history.

Although the following analysis provides a glimpse into the cultural history of American Indian peoples in San Diego County from 1850 to 1880, certain broad qualifications must be made from the onset. A crucial and primary qualification is that the data base from which this work was developed is a base with ragged edges and yawning gaps in the foundation. To a large degree, information and data provided in this paper are not reflections of what native people wrote, thought, or said. Instead, the story is one of a people who left little record of their own making or writing except as seen through the eyes of their conquerors.

Lacking transcriptions from native pens, scholars are forced to use government documents, newspaper articles, and other sources from the very people who often sought to subdue or destroy the California Indian. The authors of the material were largely white government agents, newspaper editors who wrote for a white readership, local authorities to whom the Indians posed a constant problem, and finally, Indian apologists who often misunderstood Native American culture, exaggerated the plight or condition of the natives, and wrote their views of Indian life without regard for truth or consequences. This study attempts to analyze the documents with an understanding of the era and with a critical eye toward the authors of those sources.

Acting on the suggestion of noted Indian scholar, George Harwood Phillips, this work is geared in form and structure toward the Native American order of events rather than toward a Euro-American chronology. For example, presidential eras, the Civil War, and the rise of Victorian America are of little consequence or meaning in structuring this work except as a means of providing guideposts. By virtue of the type of data available, and in an effort to structure the information into a cohesive framework, the ideal of writing an analysis explicitly and exclusively about Native Americans has given way to the reality of writing about Indian-white relations and how they affected local native peoples.

The analysis is divided into three major categories of activities by federal, state, and local governments. These three divisions are not arbitrary. They reflect the major political and economic forces that acted upon Native American civilization in the years under study, and represent three major sources of written information about the Indians of the region. A final

Indian encampment sketched by John W. Audubon, October, 1849.

qualification is one of personal judgment and interpretation. It is the primary thesis of this analysis that the Indians of San Diego County were subjected to laws, acts, and injustices as violent, racist, and inhumane as those suffered by more famous and well-chronicled Indians throughout North America. The San Diego region did not experience dramatic pitched battles, large-scale massacres, or other romantic timber for journalistic pulp mills. Cultural and physical death nonetheless took place. While the portrait may differ, the basic problems and ultimate results of white settlement and native resistance were the same locally and nationally.

As a result of using documents and resources that were generated by non-Indians, it is easier to develop a clearer picture of white reactions to, and opinions of, natives than of the natives themselves. Although such data are extremely useful in assessing white actions and toward understanding the consciousness of the dominant society, they provide little information about Native Californians **per se**. The end product of using such documents and sources is that they provide a view of American Indian history from the outside-in, a stance that imposes severe constraints on providing a history of, rather than a history about, Native Americans.

In spite of such hindrances, a picture of Native American life in the 1850-1880 period can be pieced together to form a somewhat imperfect, although hopefully, not distorted image. Yet, one is unable to provide a full rendering or depiction of a single Indian village or **rancheria** over any period of time, let alone for a populace of more than 4000 individuals for a 30-year period. Instead, the emerging portrait is a composite picture painted in broad strokes that strays not far from the truth.

A significant portion of published writings that depict the inhumanity of whites to California Indians draws examples largely from the central and northern regions. Relatively little has been written about the condition of the Indians in the southern section of the state during the period 1850- 1880. In particular, the extreme southern portion comprising modern San Diego County is rarely documented in historical works relating to Native Americans.[1] There are at least two reasons for the paucity of information about these peoples in this time period. First, the Mission Indians (as San Diego County's Indians were categorically grouped) were generally more docile than many of the more aggressive groups to the north, thus escaping specific and prolific documentation. Second, mass movements of Anglo-Americans into the gold regions of central and northern California not only had a greater, and more rapid, impact on the northern tribes, but also brought their very existence into the awareness of the invading whites.

Had the Kumeyaay (Ipai/Tipai), Luiseno, Cupeno, and Cahuilla peoples of San Diego County been eradicated or driven totally from the land, laymen and scholars alike would possibly be more aware of their story and of their suffering. Instead the academic community has been ignorant, for the most part, of the cultural deprivation, benignly unaware of American Indian presence, and, most of all, intellectually remiss in offering a portrayal of these people that implied and insisted that their plight was too much to bear and that, in response, native people crept away and died. In fact, nothing could be further from the truth.

Indian people fought the advancing tide of white settlement at all levels, using a wide variety of methods including revolt, appeasement, and cooperation. Their story is one of sadness, betrayal, neglect, and other elements that do not always sit well with the twentieth century mind. But more importantly, their story is also one of intense pride, heroic efforts, and successful adaptation, elements that the present occupants of North America consider virtues in the best tradition of Euro-American civilization. In short, these first immigrants persisted.

Chapter II

Before the Strangers:
A Prehistoric Overview

The region encompassed by present-day San Diego County contains some of the most extensive and exciting archaeological sites in the western United States. A combination of temperate climate and a varied environment from coastal seashore to rugged mountains attracted prehistoric people at a very early date. Including some disputable, 12,000 year old dates for deposits in the eastern desert area, San Diego lays claim to the most ancient remnants of these early people. The ever unfolding archaeological record includes more than 10,000 recorded sites that span at least seven millenium and perhaps as many as 12,000 years. From the first large game hunters with their bulky stone tools to those people who Spanish explorers called Dieguenos and Luisenos, the ancestors of historic San Diego left a rich legacy of rock paintings, bead work, stone architecture, finely worked tools, and other material culture that comprises an unparalleled prehistoric record.

This brief chapter provides a thumbnail sketch of prehistory for this region. The sources cited within the text are those most readily available; a review of their references will lead the reader further into the immense data base that has been produced after more than 50 years of probing and study. Table 1 provides a concise model of prehistory for the region.

The earliest documented inhabitants of San Diego County were the San Dieguito Paleo-Indians. This cultural group was first recognized by Malcolm Rogers in 1929 when he called them the "Scraper Maker Culture." Subsequent to Rogers' discovery, field work and research have led to a better understanding of San Dieguito cultural history.[1]

San Dieguito cultural history has been divided into three phases based upon technical refinements in the manufacturing of tool types. The Phase 1 San Dieguito Complex is not generally recognized as occurring west of the Laguna Mountain Range but encompassed the Mohave Desert and the area possibly as far north as Mono Lake. Conversely, the San Dieguito Phase II and III are recognized as occurring throughout San Diego County. The general artifact assemblage associated with this cultural group has been summarized.

Table 1

CHRONOLOGICAL MODEL FOR
SAN DIEGO COUNTY PREHISTORY AND HISTORY

CLIMATE	TIME	CULTURAL SETTING	STAGE
Medithermal			
Moderately warm;	1876 AD	Reservation Period	
arid and semi-	1850 AD	Anglo-European Era	
arid	1830 AD	Mexican Era	
	1769 AD	Hispanic Era	Historic
	1542 AD	Spanish Era Protohistoric	
	1000 AD	Late Prehistoric cultures	Late Milling
	3,000 BP	La Jolla Complex termination	
Altithermal	4,000 BP		
	6,000 BP		
Arid, warmer than	7,500 BP	La Jolla Complex	Early Milling
present			
Anathermal	8,000 BP	Harris Site (SDi-149) occupied	
Climate like	9,500 BP	San Dieguito Complex	Paleo-Indian
present but grow-			
ing warm, humid			
and subhumid			

- Heavy, "horse-hoof" planes
- Rounded end-scrapers, retouched by light percussion and probably hafted
- Side—and end-scrapers, probably hafted
- Choppers, made on large and heavy primary flakes
- San Dieguito Type 1 knife/points
- San Dieguito Type 2 knife/points
- Long-stemmed point/knives with weak shoulders
- Crescents
- Hammerstones
- Macro-flakes
- Thick primary flakes
- Thin trimming and finishing flakes

In a temporal context, the San Dieguito Cultural Complex has been dated relative to the initial occurrence of a later cultural group called the La Jollans. A termination date of approximately 8000 years ago for the San Dieguito can be extrapolated from radiocarbon samples obtained from the Harris Site near Rancho Santa Fe — sometimes referred to as the San Dieguito Type site — strongly indicating that these people inhabited the San Diego region at least 10,000 years ago and maybe earlier. Based on analysis of the San Dieguito artifact assemblage, most interpretations generally perceive this cultural group as game hunters. However, by 7500 years ago, the San Dieguito people had been assimilated or possibly evolved into the La Jolla Culture Complex of the Early Milling Horizon.

The Early Milling Horizon is characterized by grinding tools reflecting these people's greater dependence upon exploiting plant resources. Locally, this culture group was first described and called the "Shell Midden People" by Malcolm Rogers in 1929 and later termed the La Jolla Culture.[2] Rogers' description included two phases, La Jolla I and II, which other researchers later combined into a more comprehensive unit known as the Early Milling Horizon (also termed the Encinitas Tradition) which represented the archaeological cultures along California's southern coast. Subsequent to this definition, a technology known as the Pauma Complex was developed as a result of survey data collected in the Pauma Valley region near the San Luis Rey River. This cultural group has the characteristics of the San Dieguito and the La Jolla as exemplified by "crude, chipped stone implements and grinding stones".[3]

The La Jolla Complex is perhaps best viewed as a local cultural manifestation found along the coast and is a variant of the larger more dispersed cultural expression that includes the Pauma Complex group and is part of the Encinitas Tradition and the more generic Early Milling Horizon. The La Jolla Complex is defined by the following attributes:

- Manos and metates for processing plants
- Flexed inhumation as a burial technique
- Shell middens
- Large projectile points
- Coarsely flaked stone tools
- No pottery

The La Jolla cultural group can be interpreted as having made an ecological adaptation to shellfish and plant food as a major source for subsistence as is most clearly evident within those archaeological sites located near bays and lagoons that contained many large shell middens. This cultural complex has often been divided into three phases through use of radiocarbon dates collected from excavations with carefully controlled stratigraphy in conjunction with changes of artifact types. Consequently, the La Jolla Complex has been placed in a temporal context of approximately 7500 to 3000 years ago.

During the era of the La Jolla people's existence, significant changes were occurring in the local environment. Ocean fluctuations raised the water level and covered previously exposed dry land thus inundating many archaeological sites situated near the coast. A classic La Jolla site located near the La Jolla Beach and Tennis Club and recorded by James Moriarty in the 1960s is an example of archaeological sites submerged as a result of rising ocean waters.

Another influence from local environmental change can be observed in La Jolla sites from about 3000 years ago. Until that time, the gradual filling of many bays and lagoons with silt and sand created a favorable microenvironment for shellfish that were being exploited by the local American Indians. However, with extensive silting, the shellfish population dwindled, thus limiting the shellfish resource; a food source upon which the La Jolla were dependent. As a result, a portion of the La Jolla cultural group moved inland and adapted a subsistence economy of seed gathering and hunting. Furthermore, the diffusion of technology from peoples to the north and east assisted the La Jolla people in adjusting to their new lifestyle until the migration of the Yuman and Shoshonean cultural groups. With the arrival of these new cultures, the La Jolla gradually became assimilated.

Subsequent to amalgamation of the intruding Yuman-speaking peoples with the earlier La Jolla people circa 2000 years ago, but before the migrating Shoshonean-speaking people advanced into the area circa 1000 years ago, the development of the Late Prehistoric culture groups in San Diego County occurred. Archaeological remains from these people not only exhibit attributes similar to the Early Milling Stone Horizon (manos, metates, and flaked tools), but are also characterized by finely flaked projectile points,

Temecula Indians circa 1895 at Pechanga. Courtesy Southwest Museum.

ceramics, cremations, bedrock and portable mortars, and pictographs, as well as pit-and-groove petroglyphs.[4] An increased reliance upon an acorn-gathering economy involving particular processing techniques is clearly shown by the greater occurrence of the mortar and pestle found within these archaeological sites. The Late Prehistoric period in the northwest portion of San Diego is recognized as the San Luis Rey Complex. The complex is divided into two phases, defined as follows:

> San Luis Rey 1 is defined by the occurrence of small triangular projectile points, mortar and pestle, mano and millingstone, and simple flake scrapers. San Luis Rey II exhibits all of these plus pottery, cremation, and pictographs.[5]

In the eastern San Diego County, the Cuyamaca Complex was recognized and defined by D.L. True. Although the Cuyamaca group is similar in some traits to the San Luis Rey II cultural group, there are some attributes that are particularly characteristic of only the Cuyamaca cultural group.[6] Those characteristics are as follows:

- Cemetery areas were separated from the living areas.
- Grave markers were employed.
- Cremation ashes were placed in urns.
- Miniature vessels and shaft straighteners as well as elaborate projectile points were made for mortuary offerings.
- Many scrapers, scraper planes, and other stone tools were used extensively.

- A great variety of ceramics including specialized items such as bow pipes, effigy forms, rattles, and other forms were created.
- This culture group had a steatite industry.
- These people employed milling stone tools and other associated elements to a greater extent.
- They possibly may have had clay-lined hearths.

Ethnographically recorded Native American cultural groups in San Diego County can be considered as descended from the San Luis Rey and Cuyamaca cultural phases resulting in the Yuman-speaking Northern Diegueno (Ipai) and Southern Diegueno (Tipai-Kumeyaay) in southern San Diego and the Shoshonean-speaking Luiseno and Cahuilla in northern San Diego County.[7] The archaeological record left by these people exhibits an expanded variety of ceramic objects that are also being found in greater quantity, a greater abundance of side-notched projectile points than found associated with previous cultural groups, and a significant change in pictograph (rock painting) styles.

It was the most recent development stage of the pattern that was practiced by Indian inhabitants of San Diego when Spaniards first set foot here. Anthropologists have designated five distinguishable American Indian groups who inhabited the region at the time of contact (Refer to Figure 1). These groupings are based largely on linguistic differences rather than cultural differentiations, although some researchers have maintained that these groupings also involve variance in culture and artifacts that help set them apart. This Late Milling pattern of the Ipai, Tipai, Luiseno, Cahuilla, and Cupeno reflects cultural diversity, variable linguistic and dialectic groups, unique religious systems, and true ethnic consciousness.[8]

Cinon Duro, hereditary leader of Northern Dieguenos near Mesa Grande and Eagle Dancer, 1906. Courtesy San Diego Museum of Man.

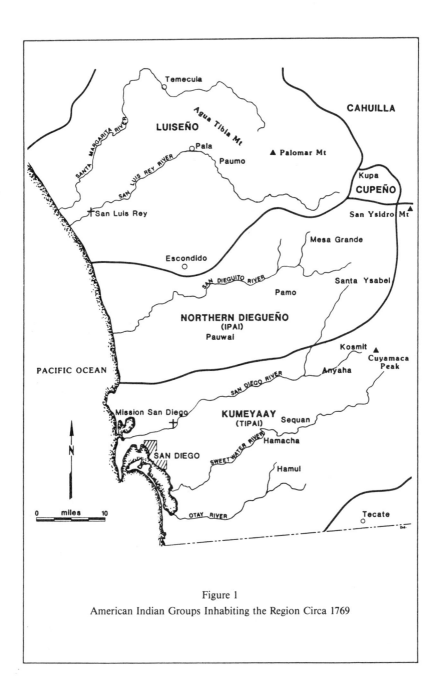

Figure 1
American Indian Groups Inhabiting the Region Circa 1769

Chapter III

Mission and Rancho:
Sowing Seeds of Destruction

With the arrival of Spanish soldiers and missionaries in San Diego, destructive forces were unleashed upon the native peoples of San Diego. Actually the movement of Franciscan priests and soldiers of the crown into Alta California, in 1769 sped up some processes set in motion by earlier exploration parties and decades of settlement in nearby Spanish borderlands. Some researchers have suggested that even those tribes situated several hundred miles from physical contact with Europeans were nonetheless infected by deadly diseases carried by native runners and traders.[1]

The arrival and settlement of Spaniards disrupted the social, economic, and cultural structure of the Indians, especially those who lived near the coast or at mission sites.[2] In the ensuing years, the affected native population was reduced by disease, conflict, and emotional abuse, sometimes intentional and other times unconscious. Controversy exists to this day regarding the motives and actions of the Franciscan fathers who colonized San Diego. Whether they were racist villians or pious men, earnestly working to "civilize" and aid the Indians, cannot be answered in this study. Whatever intent the Spanish fathers and military forces may have had, the end result was that they helped set the stage for the cultural decline and physical destruction of tens of thousands of California Indians. A shortage of women combined with the less-than-chivalrous attitudes of some Spanish soldiers caused immediate problems for Indian women. As early as 1772, Father Luis Jayme bemoaned a series of rapes that took place in nearby coastal and inland villages, including **El Corral**, near El Cajon, and **Rincon**, near Mission Bay. Jayme wrote that rapes and sexual abuse of native women was commonplace, although the soldiers were repeatedly warned and punished.[3]

European diseases took a terrible toll among the highly susceptible natives, causing a decline in the birth rate, a tremendous increase in deaths by disease and an upsurge in the incidence of crippling and debilitating illnesses.[4] Even those villages that did not have direct contact with Spaniards were nonetheless affected by the rapid spread of diseases because many travelled in the air, infecting the Indians even before whites arrived.[5] In ad-

Group of Ipai-Tipai Indians at Tecate, 1873. Courtesy Yuma County Historical Society.

dition to diseases, the Spaniards also brought cattle, horses, and sheep, animals that over-grazed lands, making the land less suitable for foraging and gathering. The animals destroyed an important segment of the Indian economy and subsistence pattern thus causing starvation.[6] In a letter dated October 17, 1772, Father Jayme wrote that Spanish soldiers had turned their animals out on the fields of the Indians who lived near the Mission San Diego and the animals "ate up their (the Indians') crops."[7] The pastoral practices of Spaniards and Mexicans, and later of Anglos, not only depleted the available grasses in and around the centers of population, but also served to drive the increasingly sparse game farther into less accessible inland valleys. The years between the arrival of Spaniards in 1769 and the Treaty of Guadalupe Hidalgo in 1848 saw a rapid decline in the coastal Indian population, movement and abandonment of villages, disintegration of moral fiber, and cultural chaos. The Indians were forced into a marginal existence in a land that had previously provided an ample supply of food and resources.[8]

The effect of the Mexican period, from roughly 1830 to 1846, on American Indians in San Diego is difficult to assess, although it appears that many of the ranch owners were cruel, insensitive masters who regarded

Indians as feudal slaves. In 1846, as Mexican domination of California ended and the American period dawned, Lieutenant William H. Emory completed an overland march to California; his diary provides a glimpse of
Indian life in this period. Arriving at John J. Warner's ranch, located north
of Santa Ysabel, Emory encountered a major Indian rancheria and found
the natives half-naked and impoverished. Although the temperature was
30 °F, the Indians did not have fires and were protected from the elements
only by their crude huts and their sheepskins. Emory commented that the
Indians lived in a form of serfdom that had been imposed on them by the
local ranch owner after the secularization of the nearby Santa Ysabel
Mission.[9]

Emory moved west toward the Pacific Ocean, encountering more Indians
at Mission San Luis Rey. Once again, the American was amazed and ap-
palled at their condition. The military officer reported that whipping was
a common form of punishing Indians and had led to several Indian deaths
for which the Mexicans responsible were never punished.[10] Summing up
his experiences at the two native villages, Emory wrote:

> This race, which in our country has never been reduced to
> slavery, is in that degraded condition thoughout California, and
> do the only labor performed in the country. Nothing can ex-
> ceed their present degraded condition.[11]

The lieutenant was not alone in recognizing the apparent despair of local
Indians under Mexican rule. Arriving in San Diego two years after Emory's
visit, Cave J. Couts camped near the rancheria of Vallecitos in the Anza-
Borrego Desert and found the Indians of that area were destitute. Couts
described their huts as hardly more than protection against the elements.[12]
Continuing west through the mountains toward Warner's Ranch, Couts
entered the rancheria of San Felipe and again remarked on the impoverished
condition of the Indians. Couts described San Felipe as "a miserable dirty
little ranche [sic] in the mountains."[13] Years later Special Commissioner
Charles A. Wetmore conducted a careful historical study and collected
numerous interviews with elderly Indians in an effort to document their
life before 1850. Wetmore concluded in 1874 that, in general, the secularization of the missions in the 1830s and the ascendancy of Mexican rule marked
the beginning of the end for the local Indians. Wetmore found that a form
of the ancient **encomienda** had existed and that "valleys which had been
the property and homes for thousands of Indian families became the property of a few landlords. From that day the Indians began to degrade.[14]
Commissioner Wetmore stated that the period following the breakup of
the mission system and that just prior to the American period was marked
by the migration of large numbers of displaced Indians from the missions

Wypooke winnowing grain, 1908. Courtesy Museum of the American Indian.

to Mexican ranchos in search of subsistence and employment. Echoing earlier statements of Emory and Couts, Wetmore stated that the natives fell into a type of feudal system that served to further dehumanize them without providing a degree of humanity usually found at the missions.[15]

Certainly the Spanish and Mexican periods set the stage for inhumane, unsavory acts that followed. Yet this in no way lessens Anglo responsibility for later attempts at native subjugation, forced removal, and eradication under the guise of democracy. Compared to Hispanic civilization, Anglo-American racial attitudes, traditional land use patterns, and economic institutions were not structured to accommodate Native Americans.[16] Thus, it is not surprising that scholars have generally agreed that Anglo settlement of California possessed a "far greater demographic impact than the Spanish-American one."[17] Following the capitulation of Mexico and the signing of the Treaty of Guadalupe Hidalgo in 1848, the American government made a moral and legal commitment to native populations (both Mexican and Indian) of the newly acquired Mexican borderlands. That the terms of the treaty, however, were rarely implemented became a fact of frontier life. According to one authority, although the treaty guaranteed property rights to the Indians of California, they were never allowed to gain legal satisfaction. As a result, the United States government denied Indians their land rights. For this reason "virtually every village was destroyed during the 1860's-1880's by aggressive Anglo entrepreneurs and ranchers."[18] While this assessment may be too generalized and somewhat overstated, at least for San Diego, the essence of the matter is that the government did not grant native populations full rights and privileges guaranteed them under the terms of the treaty. Concentrated Indian populations were particularly susceptible to Anglo violence and abuse, especially as arable land became increasingly scarce.

In prehistoric times, native people had lived in semi-permanent villages, returning to them on a seasonal basis after conducting their foraging rounds. These villages, numbering in excess of 80 throughout San Diego County, were scattered across the landscape. Generally, rancherias were located along or near major water courses, in temperate belts, in ecotones (representing the blending of differing plant communities), and in well- drained protected valleys. The Mexican period, circa 1821-1846, caused relatively greater displacement of native settlement patterns as is amply documented by George Harwood Phillips in **Chiefs and Challengers.** Phillips points out, however, that Mexican settlement patterns were also dramatically affected by Indian movement and territorial jealousy.[19] Yet, even during the Mexican period there was insufficient stimuli to draw a majority of Indians into the vortex of European pueblo life or to cause the Mexican population to impose upon the matrix of Indian life.

Chapter IV

Local Relations: Native Americans in American San Diego

The era that followed the American invasion of California in 1846-1847 was a turning point for Native Americans in San Diego County. American settlement of California created a crazy patchwork of people, motives, and success as varied as the gold rushes, land rushes, Civil War, and other justifications for making the trek to California. The years from 1848 to 1880 represent a period of rapid and profound transition in the territory that became California. The war with Mexico, the Treaty of Guadalupe Hidalgo, and the Gold Rush brought great changes to the Far West and to the San Diego area. Least mentioned in the historical literature, however, has been the profound changes that affected California's original inhabitants.

Economic and social advancement have been generally acknowledged as the primary motives for the white settlement of California. The seemingly positive reasons for the opening of the West had reverse effects upon the native populace within California. These effects are rarely addressed beyond noting that natives were displaced and many were killed. But after all, displacement and death are ascribed to the nature of the human condition, particularly on a frontier. Most traditional historians believed that conquering the so-called wilderness and taming the occupants of that uncharted land concomitant evils necessary to further the inevitable advancement of the American republic.[1] Most scholars agree that the settlement of California brought Indians living there in direct conflict with whites who generally viewed Indians as uncivilized, savage heathens. The result was racial hatred, conflict, death, and destruction.[2]

One participant in the California Indian wars was Horace Bell, an early pioneer. Bell was the archetypal, red-blooded, rough-and-ready American of western lore past and present. In his memoirs, Bell boasted of his keen ability to kill Indians, explaining proudly that he and fearless men like him would let the Indians know that they were dealing with "the invincible race of American backwoodsmen" who had already driven the Indians of North America from the land east of California and would dispense with the California Indians with equal dispatch.[3] Although Bell may have represented an extreme rather than a norm, there were more than enough of his type around to make life dangerous for thousands of California Indians. During the era from 1850-1880, the Indians lost thousands of acres of land and watched their traditional values decline because of continued sexual abuse, increased alcoholism, recurrent violence, and forced abandonment of their traditional villages. During the era, California Indians learned that justice was a concept usually extended by whites to other whites, that employment and economic opportunities were short-lived and based on the whims of white overlords, and that attempts at cultural adaptation were difficult in a white society that whimsically changed the ground rules.

Acts of violence against Indians in San Diego took many forms. Perhaps one of the most violent acts, and the one with the farthest reaching implications, was the rape of Indian girls and women. It is impossible to calculate or estimate the total number of rapes in San Diego County during the period from 1850-1880. Contemporary documents, including newspapers and diaries, indicate that rape was a fairly common occurrence, especially near the rancherias located close to white settlement. Noting that an Indian girl had been violently raped by a Mexican at Soledad, near Sorrento Valley, an editor for the **San Diego Herald** lamented in August 1853 that "We have just heard of another outrage of a similar nature committed at San Luis Rey, on a young Indian girl."[4] The editor found this particular assault especially revolting because the three **Californios** who had taken part in the rape were otherwise respectable members of the community. A year earlier, in April 1852, the same newspaper reported a series of rapes for which the editors seemed to express less compassion. The editors reported that "colored men" were drugging Indian women who "infest the town" and were indulging "their brutal.appetites."[5]

Far less violent, but nonetheless a type of sexual and emotional abuse, was the practice of white or Mexican males who would take Indian girls as temporary wives or mistresses. Whites would live with Indian women until they could find a suitable white wife or until it was time to move on in search of gold or "greener pastures." Other more designing men married Indian or Mexican women in hopes of gaining land or economic footing. This form of social mobility and marriage for sexual convenience occurred wherever lonely white men encountered friendly Indian peoples or could barter with economically depressed Indian leaders. "Squaw Man" was a universal term on the American frontier used to denote such men, and San Diego had its share of these frontier types.

A classic case of a white who married into Indian culture for convenience and long-term gain is revealed by the actions of William B. Dunn. He had been a member of the famed 1st Regiment of Dragoons under General Stephen Kearny. On the heels of the long march from Fort Leaven-

Indian men with J.J. Warner, circa 1870. Courtesy Huntington Library.

worth, Kansas, to San Diego in 1846-1847, Private Dunn decided to seek his fame and fortune in California. Shortly after his arrival, he set up housekeeping with Maria La Gradia Subria, daughter of Felipe Subria, **alcalde** of the Luiseno rancheria at Buena Vista and recipient of an 1843 land grant from the Mexican Governor, Pio Pico. By the summer of 1851, Dunn had left Maria and "taken a young squaw of tender years and has been living with her."[6] Distraught at Dunn's actions Felipe Subria accused him of raping the Indian girl and stealing his (Felipe's) land. It became all too clear to the Luiseno alcalde that Dunn intended to keep the 1184-acre wedding present of the Buena Vista Rancho and not return it as was the native custom upon rejecting one's spouse. The protests of Felipe and his daughter were ignored, thus allowing Dunn to gain control of a rancho that included parts of their ancestral rancheria. The Buena Vista Rancho itself encompassed what is now present-day Vista and the eastern margins of Buena Vista Lagoon. Dunn ultimately sold the property to Jesus

Machado, who, ironically enough, was later slain by Indians.[7]

During the 1850s, large numbers of adventurers arrived in San Diego including many single white males who took Indian wives, both legal and common-law. Such arrangements were often short-lived. The rape of Indian women and their marital business arrangements with white men caused a crisis within the Indian communities. Indian males, usually living in villages near white settlements, were often hard-pressed to find chaste brides. One Indian agent wrote, "It is almost impossible for an Indian to get a wife unless he takes one second hand."[8] Prostitution among native women was a serious problem, especially as economic conditions worsened and white settlements sprung up. Sherburne F. Cook states that native prostitution was, in some cases, a form of economic adaptation which was controlled by village leaders or by the heads of households.[9] Cook, after exhaustive studies of central and northern California, did not find any evidence for white control of Indian prostitutes nor were there any indications for it in San Diego County during that period. Local documents seem to imply that prostitution was carried out on a large scale but not in an organized sense. Native women either made their own illicit contacts or were procured by their fathers, husbands, brothers, or influential villagers. White pimping was virtually unknown. At San Pasqual, one Indian agent noted "the practice of selling young girls to white men prevailed to an alarming extent at the Rancheria."[10] Yet, because the Indians themselves were doing the selling, the agent refused to halt the practice.

The effects of sexual abuse through rape, prostitution, and short-term marriages are very difficult to assess. American Indian cultures were devastated by venereal diseases, population decline, and the loss of self esteem. Competition among Indian males for the limited number of women caused jealousy, violence, and an acute awareness among men and women that females had a new social and economic status within the larger society. The new status of women upset the traditional social and cultural equilibrium of the Indian communities.[11]

Indian men and women alike experienced Anglo abuses and violence. A variety of hostile acts were committed against Indians of both sexes, many of which were direct outgrowths of rapes, prostitution, and liquor. Although these, and other factors yet to be discussed, are crucial in understanding the declining conditions and worsening situation of Native Americans during this period, the problems caused by the affinity of certain segments of Indian society for cheap, and often fatal, liquor is a primary consideration. Although state and local laws prohibited the sale of spirits to Indians, many local merchants and traders were quick to realize the easy profits that could be made from selling low grade, easily manufactured liquor to Indians. In April 1852, Don Juan Maria Marron, Don Jose Jesus Moreno,

and the widow, Mrs. Francisco Snook of San Pasqual, were all accused
of selling liquor to the "lazy and indolent Indians" and of "keeping grog
shops near the centers of Indian activities."[12] Whether the accused were
ever convicted or even tried is not clear from available documents, although
it is unlikely they were. The fact that they were publicly accused of selling
whiskey to Indians indicates, however, the widespread concern over the sales.

Ending the sale of liquor to Indians was virtually unenforceable. The
San Diego Herald and later, the **San Diego Union**, advocated stricter enforcement of the liquor law. Influential members of the white citizenry
clamored for the same thing; yet, it was difficult to gain a conviction against
anyone accused of providing liquor to Indians. Aware that his Indian wards
were in the clutches of liquor dealers, Indian Agent Augustus P. Greene
sought to close the grog shops at San Pasqual and rid the area of the liquor nuisance. Throughout early 1870, Greene secured solid evidence
against a local dealer and actually obtained a conviction with a jail sentence
for one "notorious old offender" only to see the criminal released from
jail and absolved of the fine by San Diego County officials.[13] The effects
of Indians having easy access to cheap liquor went far beyond simple health
and economic factors. Much of the violence and degradation of Indians
living near white population centers — known as border towns — can be
directly attributed to liquor. In February 1855, three drunken Indians killed a Sonoran named Pedro Romero during a public brawl.[14] Two of the
Indians were captured and imprisoned in the San Diego jail. At the official inquest, an Indian girl, Rosaria, testified stating that the two Indian
prisoners were the men she saw attack and kill Romero. Had the alleged
assailants been white, Rosaria could not have testified. Under the California State Statutes of 1850, Chapter 133, Section 6, Indians were not allowed to testify against whites in criminal cases.[15] Because the accused were
Indians, her testimony was permitted and the two were found guilty of
murder. The guilty verdict became a moot point when the Indians made
a successful escape, one of many that were made from the San Diego jail.

Drunken, emaciated, or elderly Indians were also the targets of local
gunmen and toughs. During his temporary stint as editor of the **San Diego
Herald**, noted humorist and writer George Derby witnessed a series of
senseless shootings with Indians as the victims. In 1853 Derby wrote an
editorial using the penname, The Phoenix. He quipped that shooting Indians in south San Diego had become such a common occurrence that "we
should not be surprised at the arrival of parties from San Francisco to practice before goin' out a shootin' duels."[16] Equally bothersome to Derby and
others was the fact that whites accused of killing Indians were rarely brought
to trial and even less often convicted. The frequent failure of local judges
to prosecute the murderer of an Indian evidently carried over to Mexican

Americans as well. In December 1856, a group of thrill-seeking drunken hispanics "turned to and stoned a poor Indian, belonging to Mrs. Marone [sic] till he quietly laid down and died."[17] The **Herald** commented: "This is considered fine sport, and [if] our magistrates don't trouble themselves about such little matters, the play will be repeated."[18]

The "play" was often repeated between 1850 and 1880. In addition to the drunken brawls and frontier violence, vigilantes rose up to take the law into their hands and their primary targets were Indians. Although vigilante action was explicitly forbidden by California Statute 133, Section 11, such activities were common in the early years of San Diego County. The rationale for vigilante groups was explained by C.S. Crosby, an early Spring Valley pioneer. Complaining that white settlers were under constant harrassment from Indians from 1860 to 1870, Crosby stated that settlers took matters into their own hands because of the inaction of local law officers and because of the great distances to major white settlements. Crosby's remedy for Indian lawlessness was to make "good" Indians out of the transgressors. A "good" Indian, of course, was a dead Indian, and hanging was a favorite method of creating good Indians during the 1860s. As one authority has suggested, "if some of the sycamore trees in Jamul Valley could talk they would tell of some very queer fruit hanging from their branches."[19]

In many cases it mattered little if vigilantes administered the law directly or if the proper agencies were involved. On January 28, 1873, an Indian named Jose was jailed on a charge of grand larceny for allegedly stealing a mule belonging to Turner Helm, a local Indian-hater. During the night of January 28, or the following morning, the prisoner was taken out of jail and savagely beaten to death. The coroner's report stated that the lock on the jail had not been forced or broken and that the Indian had been removed from his cell and beaten with a blunt instrument, possibly the back of an axe.[20] Deputy Sheriff E.B. Gifford testified that earlier in the day some men had accosted him and "several made the remark, that the cheapest way to get rid of the son of a bitch was to take him out and hang him."[21] Jose's death certificate was notable for its brevity, stating that Jose was Indian, twenty-eight years of age, and had died as the result of assassination on or about January 29, 1873.[22] The sheriff filed no charges against Jose's slayers.

At least three cases of imprisoned Indians, who may have been hung while in custody, appear in contemporary documents. On June 6, 1875, an Indian named Sole was found hanged to death in his cell. He had been drunk and disorderly when arrested and had been bound with rope prior to and during his imprisonment.[23] Whether Sole loosened his bonds and then hanged himself or was lynched by economy minded vigilantes will never

CABEZON
Leader of the Desert Cahuilla, 1890.
Courtesy Southwest Museum.

be known. Likely, vigilantes hanged the Indian. In any case, reacting to Sole's death and recalling the assasination of Jose two years before, a delegation of fifty to sixty Indians assembled in Julian on June 12, 1875 to protest. The Indians complained that they feared for the safety of their men in the local jail even when locked up for minor crimes. After a heated exchange with white officials, the Indians left town assured that an official inquiry would be held.[24] The subsequent official coroner's report stated that Sole died by hanging while in jail. No circumstances were mentioned and no guilt was implied.[25]

Two other cases of Indian hangings while in jails, either from their own acts or from whites, occurred in September 1875 and in November 1880. The hanging in 1875 claimed the life of a Sonoran Indian who, the official clerk noted, died from loss of breath.[26] The Indian hanged to death in 1880 was a local who reportedly committed suicide while in jail and was buried in the San Diego County cemetery.[27] The Julian City Jail in particular was not known for its protection of Indian prisoners. The deaths of Jose and Sole were not isolated incidents. On June 23, 1878, an Indian named Juan de Cruz was arrested for allegedly stabbing Mrs. George V. King Banner, wife of the well-known pioneer whose name is retained in the Banner Grade Road. Cruz was picked up and charged with the crime. During the night of June 23, a crowd of men entered the jail, subdued guard William Woods (who by his own admission offered only token resistance) and kidnapped the prisoner. A coroner's report noted that Juan de Cruz was found dead in an adjacent field. The cause of death was strangulation inflicted "by parties unknown."[28] Law enforcement officials made no attempt to learn the identity of the kidnappers. According to the court records, the guard was not even asked if he could identify the man who had subdued him.

The years from 1877 to 1878 were dangerous ones for most non-European minorities in San Diego County. As is often the case during times of stress or adverse conditions, it is the minorities who are scapegoated, becoming the object of physical abuse and violence. Within the San Diego City limits, a series of anti-Chinese riots flared up, resulting in the maiming of several Chinese.[29] The severe drought of 1877 caused tempers to rise, and men sought relief at the expense of Chinese and Indians. The Indians, who controlled valuable water sources, were singled out and attacked. The region surrounding Warner's Hot Springs was especially affected by the drought. Local Anglos, including Chatham Helm and his brother Turner Helm, sought every means possible to get water to their livestock and crops. Aware that Indians of the area were also suffering, Helms regularly patrolled the canyons and valleys in search of stray livestock to make sure that the Indians did not rustle them, as some Indians did during hard times. While riding near the Hot Springs in August 1877, a group of Dieguenos had the misfortune of encountering Chatham Helm and some of his comrades who were riding the range. The Indians and whites exchanges hostile words, and Helm became agitated. Rifles flashed, and moments later at least one Indian, Francisco, lay dead in the blowing dust.

Testimony during the coroner's inquest revealed that Chatham had blocked the Indians' passage and then became beligerent with them. A witness testified that Chatham had brandished his rifle, saying: "I want to kill an Indian today."[30] The witness could not recall if the Indians began to disperse or if they simply stood their ground. Regardless, within seconds a rifle shot pierced the air, and Francisco slumped to the ground. Chatham Helm reportedly shouted that he had shot and killed an Indian. However, officials conducting the inquest found that "the deceased came to his death by a gunshot wound being inflicted by some party unknown."[31] Helm was never indicted or even questioned regarding the death of Francisco. Proudly brandishing a tomahawk wound received while fighting Plains Indians, Helm continued his harrassment of the Hot Springs Indians until his death. As late as 1887, the Cahuillas still feared the Helms who had homesteaded on their lands. Fearing reprisals and more killings, the Cahuillas allowed Helm to claim the land by default.

While life on the frontier in the mid-nineteenth century might have been hazardous, it was particularly so for Native Americans. After a highly romanticized trip through San Diego County, author and activist, Helen Hunt Jackson, summed up the degree to which Native Americans were subjected to violence. "The Indians' own lives are in continual danger, it being safe to shoot an Indian at any time when only Indian witnesses are present."[32] In addition to being victims of vigilante action and outright violence, Indians, as is often the case with minorities, were also convenient scapegoats for all forms of white accusations. In December 1879, a group of white juveniles were arrested for taking part in a wave of thefts that had plagued San Diego. Their arrest finally exonerated local Indians who had automatically been accused of the acts. The **San Diego Union** noted that although Indians were starving, they had not taken part in this series of thefts as was commonly suspected.[33] On another occasion, white citizens blamed and harassed Indians for the deeds of an organized band of Mexican horse thieves. Having lost a considerable number of horses, local ranchers near San Pasqual assumed that they had been victims of Indian thievery and began planning their reprisals. They planned to punish local Indians severely, until they found the horses in the possession of Mexican outlaws. Only then were the Indians absolved of guilt and out of danger from vigilante ranchers.[34]

The inequity of law enforcement for Native Americans was especially pronounced. In the 1870s, a Mexican named Claudio killed Ensico, an Indian, at San Pasqual. In this instance the Indian was well-known and respected for his carpentry skills. This, along with the fact that the alleged killer was a Mexican, probably ensured that Claudio was brought to trial. A jury of six whites and six Mexicans found Claudio guilty and put him under armed guard until he could be transported to San Diego. Claudio never served a day of his sentence. As a pioneer noted, "In the night he got away and was never seen in the valley again in daylight."[35]

Indian rancherias near white settlements became hodgepodge collections of tattered huts, evil odors, and barking dogs. Within these squalid confines lived the destitute and forgotten elders, Indian outlaws, and Native Americans who were forced to eke out a tenuous, parasitic life similar to that of the age-old camp followers. Well aware of the poor conditions in local Indian rancherias, a San Diego Grand Jury made the recommendation in 1852:

> A removal of the numerous Rancherios (without exception) should be ordered, as they are not only an eyesore, but the hiding place of idle and pilfering Indians. None of these remnants of a degenerate age should be allowed on this side of the river.[36]

Ultimately, the grand jury had its way, and Indians were gradually pushed out of the city into remote canyons and tidelands where they again tried to continue their lives unmolested.

Even after major concentrations of Indians moved away from white settlements, large numbers of Indians continued to drift into towns and villages in search of employment and liquor. In an effort to rid the streets and alleys of undesirables of all races, the city passed Section 1 of City Ordinance 5 which made unlawful the act of public intoxication.[37] At least twelve Indians were arrested and convicted of being publicly intoxicated between August 1874 and June 1878. The usual fine for these Indians was between five and ten dollars, the same as that for whites or Mexicans convicted of the same crime.[38] Indians who lacked the cash to pay their fines were sentenced to jail at a rate varying from one dollar a day to fifty cents a day. One Indian chief was released without fine or imprisonment while another was bailed out by a local rancher. One individual paid the court when he had the money toward the end of the month. Based on data from the years 1874 to 1883, it does not appear that paroled Indians were forced into any type of indentured servitude or other repressive measures as was the case in Los Angeles County.[39] It is possible that by the 1870s and 1880s this practice had been abandoned in San Diego County. Data from earlier periods are too fragmentary to draw any firm conclusions about indenture in those years, although it certainly existed to some degree.

Besides administering the intoxication act, white officials had other direct contacts with nearby Indians. In an effort to cope with starving and homeless Indians, the County of San Diego occasionally afforded them indigent status. As with most of the measures established to aid Native Americans, the county's efforts to aid indigents were rather insincere and non-productive. As early as 1853, M.M. Sexton, San Diego County Sheriff, wrote the Board of Supervisors that a group of old and blind Indians were known to be without food or adequate shelter on the outskirts of San Diego. Sexton reported that he could not assist them and requested that the supervisors provide some form of relief.[40] Whether the supervisors aided the Indians at this time is not known, although the request illustrates the problem and suggests that some officials demonstrated a concern. In the 1870s, the county often paid for the construction of a coffin and the burial of dead, indigent natives. One such case involved "an Indian boy who had died and is not able to get a coffin."[41] The supervisors recommended that a local coffin maker provide a suitable coffin for the indigent youth. A deceased Indian woman did not fare so well in January 1874. The **San Diego Union** noted that three Indian women had died the preceding week and that one women was buried in blankets at the old Presidio de San Diego because a coffin was not available.[42]

The precise reason for burial of Indians in the abandoned Catholic cemetery on Presidio Hill is not clear, although it was likely used because it was the site of Presidio Chapel, and the cemetery held religious significance for converted Indians. Recent archaeological investigation and contemporary documents indicate that the use of the old presidio **campo santo** as an Indian burial ground was fairly common from 1850 to 1875. At least five Indians were buried on Presidio Hill between 1873 and 1875 alone, although it is possible that additional burials went unnoticed by local authorities.[43] Whatever the reasons for burying Indians on Presidio Hill, it does not appear that whites forced it upon them in an effort to segregate local cemeteries. During the 1870s, Indians were also buried in the San Diego County cemetery, the San Diego City cemetery, and at the **campo santo** in Old Town.[44] Indians fared better than the Chinese who were not permitted to bury their dead in public cemeteries but rather "on the hill" or in the "China burial place."[45] Although the county incurred the cost of coffins and burials for some indigent Indians and may have, on occasion, offered them some relief, the money came, at least in part, from an "Indian Fund" created by pooling the surplus fines and debts of convicted Indians. In one such case, Justice of the Peace W.H. Noyes certified on November 2, 1858 that Jose, a local Indian, was convicted of petty larceny and fined twenty-five dollars. Lacking the funds to pay the fine, Jose was ordered to sell his saddle and other personal goods. The difference between the fine, the court costs, and the amount raised by the sale of his goods was one dollar, which Noyes reported would go into the Indian fund for later use.[46]

Indians encountered economic and social obstacles in San Diego County. Prostitution, theft, drunkenness, and jail sentences were often the result of the low economic and social status of Indians. Unable to continue their traditional way of life and economic pursuits, many Native Americans adapted to the economic system of the dominant society and sought employment. Between 1850 and 1870, about the only employment opportunities open to Indians were those generally open to immigrants or persons considered socially or racially inferior. Whites and Hispanics employed Indians as day laborers in unskilled capacities or as domestics and herders. Although not directly applicable to San Diego Indians, there is truth to Albert Hurtado's statement that "instead of resisting the whites, restricting settlements, and impeding development, California Indians worked obediently in the whites' fields and houses in return for food and shelter."[47]

On special occasions, large numbers of Native Americans were used as menial labor on construction projects such as the building of the Derby Dike in 1853. For this ill-fated project, whites hired at least 100 Indians to help divert the San Diego River from its original flood channel through Old Town. The Indians received $15.00 per month, tent housing, and some basic foodstuffs.[48] In contrast, white laborers received $60.00 per month on the same job. To keep the Indians in line, Lt. George Derby hired Manuelito Cota, the white-appointed captain general of the Luiseno Indians, and Old Tomas, who had been recently deposed as **alcalde** of the Mesa Grande Indians. Besides serving as a labor foreman, Manuelito was also hired as a tracker of both man and beast. A **San Diego Herald** article dated November 11, 1854 reported that Manuelito was out tracking bandits in hope of garnering reward money.[49] Whites hired other Indians as trackers, including Jose, an Indian resident of Old Town, known for his ability to track deer. His career as a tracker ended on January 7, 1875, when he was murdered behind the Cosmopolitan Hotel.[50] An inquest concluded that he was slain by persons unknown.

Throughout the late 1850s and 1860s, whaling schooners put into port at San Diego, taking on Native Americans as ship hands. The early 1860s were boom years for whalers and schooners such as the **Eagle** and **Sarah MacFarland**, and the ship owners regularly employed both natives from San Diego and from the Sandwich Island (Hawaii).[51] However, more typical of the work done by Indians was their use as herders. Cave J. Couts, the Indian subagent for San Diego County, had at least fifteen Indian herders working for him at Rancho Guajome and noted that the Luisenos "are the main dependence of our rancherios for vaqueros."[52] B.D. Wilson voiced much the same thought when he said:

> The Indian laborers and servants were domesticated; mix with
> us daily and hourly; and, with all their faults, appear to be a
> necessary part of the domestic economy. They are almost the
> only source of farm servants we have.[53]

Regarding the reliability of Indians as herders and vaqueros, Tamar E.M.
Bevington, an early pioneer woman at San Pasqual, related that John
Wolfskill trusted Indian herders more than whites or Californios.[54] Between 1875 and 1887, local Indians at San Pasqual hired on to fill a variety
of positions. Mrs. Bevington noted that the Indians of the area liked her
husband and that they "would come and work for him whenever he asked
them to. And I hired them to wash and help about the house."[55] In his
report of 1874, Special Commissioner Charles A. Wetmore stated that life
was precarious for the Indian inhabitants of San Diego County and that
they were forced to wander from rancho to town seeking employment. Wetmore found their employment less than satisfactory and stated that, "they
pick grapes, herd and wash sheep, chop wood, and do ordinary menial service."[56] Indians worked on ranches throughout the county. In the Spring
Valley area, Judge Augustus S. Ensworth hired Indians to work his spread.
Ironically, Ensworth had built his adobe ranchhouse in the center of the
recently abandoned Tipai village of **Neti** or **Meti**. This important village
was a leader in the 1775 attack on Mission San Diego de Alcaía. Ensworth
paid his Indian employees a dollar a day.[57] Further south in National City, Charles Kimball, the founder of National City, noted in his diary of
1877 that he had hired two Indian laborers for ten dollars apiece per month
plus board.[58]

George McKinstry, a popular northern San Diego County doctor and
farmer, reported in 1860 that at least twelve Luiseno Indians were cutting
wheat and hauling barley in the Mesa Grande area.[59] In October 1880,
McKinstry reported that north county Indians were making adobes for
chimneys and building a kitchen for the house of George Dyke.[60] Other
Indians worked as messengers, vaqueros, general laborers, and kitchen help.
A neighbor of McKinstry, Joseph Foster, frequently hired Indian boys as
messengers and sheep herders. Between 1874 and 1880, he hired several Indians to shear and herd his livestock as a means of paying his poll tax, Foster
assigned Indians to work on county road projects.[61] Foster's rates of pay
were equitable for the time. In March 1877, he paid an Indian 4-1/2 cents
a head to shear sheep, and he paid two Indians $1.50 for less than a day's
work for his poll tax. He also hired one Indian semi-permanently for $.50
a day and paid an Indian boy $15.50 for about 58 days of labor.[62] Foster's
main source of Indian labor was Capitan Grande and the Indian villages

Indian Fiesta at Santa Ysabel, circa 1914. Courtesy San Diego Historical Society.

in and around Ballena Valley near Ramona. Although Foster constantly had thousands of sheep roaming the hills near Indian rancherias, the white man never mentioned an infraction or act of violence against himself or his property during the years 1874 and 1880. Foster's dealings with the Indians seem to have been based on fair play and a desire to live amicably with his Indian neighbors.

San Diego entrepreneur Ephraim W. Morse hired scores of Indians to labor in his mines in Baja California. He hired Indians from local Baja California tribes to work as miners and messengers to run correspondence back to San Diego. Whiskey and the stigma of drunken Indians were prevalent down south also. An anonymous labor foreman for Morse noted in his diary that on September 17, 1865 there was a "big drunk down at the adobe makers camp. Had to drive off Indians and Mexicans from camp."[63] The foreman found drunk Indians troublesome but placed the blame on the whites who made their living selling cheap whiskey to Indians. The foreman wrote, "these d—d people are bringing liquor all the time, now, to sell to Indians, causing serious interruption to our regular work."[64] Although some specific information is available on employment patterns for adult Indians, it is difficult to document the quantity or type of work done by Indian children. Many households that listed Indian servants also listed Indian children, presumably the offspring of the adult domestics.[65] These children likely helped with the herding, wood chopping, sweeping, cleaning or whatever task the employer asked them to do.

Besides work for hire and normal forms of employment, a type of indentured servitude developed in early San Diego. It was general policy that
Indians who were unlucky enough to be jailed or convicted of a crime were
put to work on labor gangs or parceled out to local ranchers in return for
their bail. This practice was so common in Los Angeles that white officials
held regular Sunday auctions to clear out the jails after a festive Saturday
night. In San Diego, Judge Joseph Leonard sentenced Indians to some form
of labor rather than to "hard" jail time, without actually indenturing them.
It is to the credit of Judge Leonard that his fines or sentences for Indians
were consistent with those meted out to whites and Mexicans.[66] Although
indenture for adults seems to have been limited to short-term service in
lieu of jail, there are indications that young Indians were frequently indentured out to white families. In one case, A.J. Chase of San Francisco related
to Ephraim Morse, in a letter dated June 2, 1866, that a friend of Chase,
Mr. Rosekrans, sought an Indian girl aged seven and a half as an indentured servant. Evidently, Morse and Chase had been involved in setting up
the transfer of other Indian children, because Chase said that Rosekrans
would take the new girl "on the same condition we made with Mrs.
Maxcy."[67] Later that summer, Rosekrans decided against taking an indentured servant, forcing Chase to write Morse and explain that Rosekrans
had made some other specified arrangements and no longer wanted the
Indian girl.[68]

In one case, a child eight years old was indentured to Joseph Smith of
San Diego. At the court hearing, Justice of the Peace William H. Noyes
noted that the child, Frederico, appeared with his parents, Augustine and
Ramona. No coercion was evident. The official indenture document authorized Smith to "have the care, custody, control and earnings of said Frederico,
minor, until he obtains the age of fifteen years."[69] The circumstances
leading to Frederico's indenture are unknown. His parents may have literally
sold him into bondage for cash or to pay off a debt to Smith. It is also
possible that Smith offered to take care of the child in hopes that he could
labor on the Smith's ranch in return for a chance for Frederico to learn
a trade. Whatever the particulars, there is fragmentary evidence that a type
of indentured servitude was practiced in San Diego County and that children
were involved in the manner described above.

Of 2692 Indians listed in the 1860 census for San Diego County, 106 were
noted as having an occupation.[70] Examination of that census reveals that
42 Indians were listed as laborers, 20 as servants, 7 females were listed as
washerwomen, 22 males were vaqueros, 4 were noted as cooks, and 1 each
was recorded as gardener, woodpacker, and shepherd. It should be
remembered that these are from a census that did not list the entire population or spectrum of occupations then existing in San Diego County, such

as whalers, farmers, and craftsmen. The census did not include all of the Indians in 1860, only 25 were included in the census. Assuming at least one-half of the Indian villages were recorded, a population of approximately 4000 appears accurate. Table 2 shows overall native population figures for 1860-1879 as they appeared in official documents, and Table 3 contains population data for 31 of the major villages in San Diego County.[71]

In general, it seems reasonable to assume that those Indians who could find employment were holding poor-paying, low-status jobs that could be, and were, terminated at the whim of Anglo employers. Based on this, it can be inferred that — with few exceptions — most Indians did not possess the chance to establish primary relationships with the socially-aloof Anglos, or gain much from white contact. Addressing himself to the plight of Native Americans who lived with white families, Judge Benjamin Hayes wrote in 1861:

> This seems to be a hard fate for that race [Indian] — that there cannot be in a [white] family sufficient tenderness and a degree of education, to wean them from the taste for returning to the habits of their tribes. Perhaps, there are too many influences now working against any sensible improvement of their condition.[72]

In 1875, Special United States Commissioner Charles A. Wetmore reported that the employment of Indians was just a niche above blacks held in slavery:

> ...they easily fell into the occupations offered by the rancheros, who needed vaqueros and menials for their vast estates. This feudal life, into which the Indians were forced by circumstances, was less civilizing than the mission life of the past. They were no longer instructed in the useful arts, but were used and debauched at the pleasure of their master.[73]

From a historical perspective, the patterns that Hayes and Wetmore describe were the last vestiges of the old Hispanic system of encomiendas and repartimientos. Except now the Indians were expected to toil for white private landowners not for the church or state. With nearly 100 years of near-feudal experiences behind them, it may have been easy to comply with the new landlords' wishes, at least at first.

Had the Anglos robbed Native Americans of their rich culture and replaced it with an intelligible alternative or taught Indians some elements of white culture, Indians could have coped in the era of great social and cultural upheaval. Instead, whites took what they wanted, causing a rapid decline in native morale and economic fiber. As Wetmore, Hayes, and other

Table 2

SAN DIEGO COUNTY NATIVE AMERICAN POPULATION
(1860-1880)

Source	Native Group			
				Total Including Unspecified
	Luiseno	Diegueno	Cahuilla	
Census – 1860	NS	NS	NS	2,692
Lovett – 1865	—	1,400	—	1,400
Stanley – 1867	—	600	—	NS
McIntosh – 1869	600	1,500	1,200	3,300
Greene – 1870	1,299	2,500*	1,257	5,056
Ames – 1873	972	NS	1,000	4,000**
Smith – 1874	NS	NS	NS	5,000**
Wetmore – 1875	NS	NS	NS	2,500
Smith – 1875	NS	NS	NS	4,000
Colburn – 1877	NS	NS	NS	4,000
Lawson – 1879	NS	NS	NS	3,000*
Jackson – 1880	1,120	675	731	2,526

*Estimated.
**Includes San Bernardino.
 NS: Not Stated.

Table 3

POPULATIONS OF SELECTED SAN DIEGO COUNTY NATIVE SETTLEMENTS

(1852-1873)

Native Settlement Dieguenos	Wilson 1852	Census 1860	Hayes 1862	Lovett 1864	Greene 1870	Uback 1873	Ames 1873
San Dieguito	20	—	—	—	—	—	—
San Diego Mission	20	59	—	—	—	—	—
San Pasqual	75	133	—	—	195	200	—
Jamacha	100	—	—	—	—	—	—
Santa Ysabel	100	185	—	—	—	200	125
San Jose de Valle	100	67	—	—	—	—	—
Mataguay	75	34	—	—	—	80	—
Lorenzo	30	—	—	—	—	—	—
San Felipe	100	73	—	—	—	50	—
Cajon	50	—	—	—	—	—	—
Cuyamaca	50	—	—	—	—	—	—
Valle de los Viejos	50	—	—	—	—	—	—
Mesa Grande	—	122	—	—	—	100	—
Mesa Chiquita	—	19	—	—	—	36	—
Guatay	—	46	—	—	—	50	—
Capital Grande	—	64	—	—	—	50	—
Agua Caliente[1]	—	156	254	148	—	200	168
TOTALS:	770	958	ID	ID	195	986	ID

Native Settlement Luisenos							
Pauma	—	90	120	106	—	100	—
Potrero	—	118	310	177	—	400	—
San Ysidro	—	65	50	90	—	24	—
Pala	—	143	155	162	137	100	—
Aguanga	—	34	16	85	—	56	—
La Jolla (Apuche)	—	92	112	175	—	300	—
Yapitchah (Rincon)	—	60	53	—	—	—	—
Puerta Chiquita	—	20	20	80	—	—	—
Puerta de la Cruz	—	54	58	84	—	50	—
Coyotes	—	14	120	140	—	—	—
Vallecito	—	30	20	—	—	100	—
Saboba	—	119	—	130	—	—	—
San Luis Rey	—	107	—	75	—	—	—
Temecula	—	323	300	382	—	200	—
TOTALS	—	1,269	1,334	1,686	137	1,324	—
TOTAL BOTH GROUPS:	—	2,227				2,310	

[1]Mixed Village (Diegueno & Luiseno).   ID: Insufficient Data.

socially aware people realized, Indians were forced to depend upon an inhospitable core society for their economic subsistence and were, at the same time, left without the religious and moral guides possessed by their parents and grandparents. American Indians in San Diego County were left in limbo, caught between a rich, cultural past and a bleak, dismal future.

Chapter V

Separate and Unequal:
Legalizing the Dispossession

Following California statehood in 1850, state legislators faced the enormous task of establishing and codifying a body of state laws. Besides the more obvious needs, such as tax codes, legislative procedures, and civil codes, legislators decided to establish laws and regulations dealing specifically with the large Native American population, totaling more than 30,000 persons. Previously most injustices against Californian Indians were spawned locally and were frequently not legally codified, the state government prescribed a series of laws and statutes that were, for the most part, official, legal sanctions for white abuses of natives.

Any assessment of legal systems and Indian policies requires an understanding of the ability or inability of government to maintain and enforce those laws. The enforcement, interpretation, and ultimate value of any law or governmental edict was only as viable as the law enforcement agency. Federal and state law officers throughout the period from 1850 to 1880 exerted a minimal amount of control and influence over the lives of whites and Indians alike. Passage of laws that were overtly anti-Indian was hardly unique to California or to the western states. California apparently was no better or worse than the thirty states that preceded it into statehood. Most legislators from 1850 to 1880 were recent immigrants who brought their own preconceived ideas of race, superiority, and legal justice to California. In his study of the California character, historian Josiah Royce suggested that early immigrants had "a diseased local exaggeration of our common national feeling toward foreigners ... a hearty American contempt for things and institutions and people that were stubbornly foreign."[1] California laws, passed between 1850 and 1880, possess strong similarities to anti-Indian doctrines practiced by both state and federal governments prior to and during this period.

Charles S. Cushing, an early twentieth century legal analyst, noted that California's first constitution and basic laws were simple stereotypes of existing laws in other areas.[2] California legislators attempted to blend the more urbane and sophisticated legal tracts of the eastern states with the no-nonsense frontier code of the western states. What resulted was a strange

Table 4

EXCERPTS FROM CALIFORNIA STATE STATUTES CHAPTER 133: "AN ACT FOR THE GOVERNMENT AND PROTECTION OF INDIANS"

SUMMARY OF SECTION	SECTION NO.
Justices of the Peace shall have jurisdiciton in all cases of complaints by and against Indians	Section 1
Current landowners shall allow Indians to continue living on lands now occupied by them; forced abandonment prohibited	Section 2
Rights of custody and control of Indian children during their minority can be assumed by whites	Section 3
Penalties provided for neglect of Indian wards	Section 4
Justice of the Peace shall bind Indians and whites to contracts	Section 5
Whites shall not be convicted of offense based on the testimony of an Indian	Section 6
Indian fund established to disposal of fees and fines levied against Indians	Section 8
Setting fire to grasslands prohibited	Section 10
Indians sentenced to pay fines may be compelled to work off fine and court costs through bondage to a white person	Section 14
Sale of intoxicating liquors to Indians strictly prohibited	Section 15
Indians convicted of theft of livestock, horses or other valuables, shall be lashed	Section 16
Able-bodied Indians who are unemployed, loitering, begging or unable to support themselves shall be considered as vagrant and hired out for a term not exceeding four months	Section 20

mixture of Jeffersonian and Jacksonian democracy. The ambiguity, injustice, and racial implications of similar laws and attitudes beyond California are discussed in other historical and legal studies.[3] Furthermore, it is instructive to read and compare the Black Codes of the American South with the various California Indian Acts to understand the malevolent nature of early California law in a broader historical-legal context. Analysis by Ferdinand Fernandez serves as a basis for the following discussion which is necessarily brief, owing to the clarity and thoroughness of his study.[4] Pertinent state laws passed in 1850 that affected Native Americans are shown in Table 4.

In April 1850, the California legislature passed California Statute Chapter 133, as a body of laws entitled "An Act for the Government and Protection of Indians." Through this act, the state established a body of rules and regulations that directly affected California Indians, usually negatively. Although amendments and adaptations were added throughout the years, this act remained fundamentally the same until the late 1880s. For the most part, these laws sought to regulate Indians at the state level rather than protect them, a direct challenge to the United States Supreme Court decision of 1832, (**Worcester vs. Georgia**). Section 1 of Chapter 133 invested local justices of the peace with the power and authority to preside over all cases of complaints both for and against Indians.[5] While ensuring that local officials could deal with Indian problems, thus expediting law enforcement and providing for local autonomy, Section 1 also placed enormous power in the hands of men who were often anti-Indian. Lacking formal directives and procedures for applying the Protection Act, justices of the peace were left to their own measures.

Section 2 of Chapter 133 was a positive effort on the part of the state to guarantee at least limited Indian land rights. In summary, Section 2 stated that Indians currently residing on public or private lands be allowed to continue their residence unmolested.[6] Although making it illegal to remove Indians, Section 2 did not acknowledge the principle of Indian land ownership as much as it forbade disruption of their peace without due process. Section 3 of the 1850 statutes legalized the already widespread practice of whites assuming custody of Indian children. In an attempt to discourage the widespread kidnapping of Indian children, Section 3 stressed that a legal certificate was required to ensure that children were not being forced into servitude against the wishes of their parents. In a further attempt to halt mistreatment of Indian minors, the legislature of 1850 passed Section 4, which made it illegal to mistreat indentured Indian children through neglect of food or clothing. The fine for such abuse was $10.00, a penalty rarely applied.

Indenture was not limited to Indian minors. Section 5 of the acts of 1850

Indian woman with burden basket, circa 1890. Courtesy Yuma County Historical Society.

provided for binding of adult Indians to labor contracts upon approval of justices of the peace.[7] Ostensibly, this law provided California Indians a chance to gain experience and trade skills. In application, this law served as a legal means to bind Indians to contracts that they seldom desired or understood. The intent and effect of Section 5 is perhaps better understood when one realizes that the same California legislators adopted Fugitive Slave Laws for blacks in keeping with the Black Codes practiced in the South. Section 20 of the statutes was closely related to Section 5 and to the Fugitive Slave Laws. Seemingly endowed with an overzealous Protestant work ethic, California legislators sought to ensure that no able-bodied person stood idle. Section 20 stated that any vagrant Indian should be arrested.[8] The definition of vagrancy was vague and oriented toward an Anglo concept of wealth and residency. It was not difficult "to charge anyone with vagabondage, especially by enlisting the potent aid of liquor, and obtain his condemnation to forced labor."[9] Although vagrancy laws were applied to all races, Indians were categorically exempted from the statute defining a vagrant as one who went 10 days without employment.

Native Californians jailed for vagrancy and unable to post bail were subject to the provisions of Section 14 of Chapter 133. One of the most injurious laws of 1850, Section 14, stated that a white could post bond for incarcerated vagrant Indians. In return, Indians were required, by state statute and local practice, to work for their white benefactors for a duration and pay rate established by Anglos.[10] The direct consequence of Section 14 was that thousands of Native Americans were legally made wards of white individuals who sought a cheap and steady labor supply. Throughout the 1850s and 1860s, Los Angeles County auctioned Indian prisoners, providing whites with near-slave labor. In separate studies of the Indian indenture system, two scholars concluded that the system as practiced from 1850 to 1865 was racist, dehumanizing, widespread, and frequently implemented.[11] The frequency of this system in San Diego County is difficult to ascertain, although it was certainly practiced.

Indians involved in alleged violations, including vagrancy, were at the mercy of the Anglo judicial structure. Cultural differences, language barriers and reluctance of Indians to indulge in conversation often served as indications of guilt to Anglo courts. Section 6 of Chapter 133 disallowed Indian testimony against whites. This section stated that no white person could be convicted of any offense on the testimony of an Indian.[12] The following year, the California legislature excluded Indians from applying for admission to the California bar.[13] Unable to testify and unable to have native legal counsel, Indians were totally dependent upon whatever legal assistance, usually none, whites offered. The effects of these laws were noted by Helen H. Jackson in a governmental report filed in 1886. Jackson

reported that Indians throughout southern California were at the complete
mercy of white-dominated courts and laws and the much heralded American
legal system was a weapon to be used against native peoples.[14] Indians
convicted of theft involving horses, cattle, or other items considered valuable
were, according to Section 16 of the 1850 act, subject to public floggings.[15]
In essence, this law merely legalized the ruthless **modus operandi** of local
vigilantes and sheriffs, although it did stipulate that no more than twenty-
five lashes could be applied. Fifteen years later, the Supreme Court of
California declared that flogging was cruel and unusual punishment, and
ruled the act unconstitutional.[16]

Two additional laws passed in 1850 were aimed at decreasing Indian
disruptions of Anglo society. Section 10 made it illegal to set or fail to ex-
tinguish brush fires.[17] While of obvious benefit to cattlemen and farmers,
this law made it unlawful for Native Americans to practice an ancient hunting technique, capturing small game by setting fire to grasslands and herding game either into canyons or over mesa tops. Section 15 forbade anyone
from selling alcohol to Indians. In spite of the prohibition of the sale of
liquor to Indians, liquor was easily accessible to Native Americans, thus
assuring a steady flow of drunken vagrants from street gutters to jails. If
anything, the anti-liquor law made Indians more reliant upon unscrupulous
grog shop owners and merchants who hovered around Indian rancherias
selling toxic, low-grade liquor. Throughout the years from 1851 to 1880,
the California legislature passed, enacted, and repealed many laws dealing
specifically with Native Americans. For the most part, these laws were based
on the patently anti-Indian statutes of 1850 and, as such, were laws that
sought to keep natives in their place while ensuring that whites would
not be bothered by the remnants of the original occupants of southern
California.

Even laws and decrees that appear to lessen control over Indians or ex-
tend rights to them frequently had an opposite effect if not intent. In 1865,
the Supreme Court of California decreed that the 1850 Statute for the
Punishment and Protection of Indians did not apply to Indians living
among whites.[18] At first appearance, the decree of 1865 seemed to end Indian indenture to whites. In fact, it simply exempted white ranchers from
compliance with the statute while affording Indians no more protection.
In essence, while punishment of so-called "civilized" Indians was left to
local jurisdictions, the protection of such Indians was eliminated. In addition to laws that sought to punish Indians for specific crimes against the
white community, the California legislature also passed laws that limited
the ability of the Indians to assert, educate, or defend themselves. As is
the case with the Indian population today, they were forced to adhere to

Interior of Indian home at Mesa Grande, circa 1890. Courtesy Bancroft Library.

a body of laws above and beyond the regulations that all citizens of California were obligated to respect.

In 1854, the California legislature passed Section 1, Chapter 12 of the state statutes. This act prohibited the sale of any firearms or ammunition to any California Indian or to persons known to associate with Indians.[19] Coupled with the earlier anti-brush fire law, these laws left Indians without a viable means of hunting. White encroachments and over-exploitation of game had long since made bow and arrow hunting inefficient. The anti-gun law also imposed an intentional disarming of Indians at a period in history when virtually every frontier community was ripe with gunfights and trigger-happy Indian haters. This act was repealed in 1913 after several decades of social conflict.

The benefits of, and need for, education have frequently been considered an integral part of the American system and the American success story. Whites advocated that Indians should become "civilized" and "Americanized," at the same time they passed legislation excluding Indians from white schools. As early as 1855, California established the legal basis for exclusion of minorities from California schools. Known as the "Common School Act," this piece of legislation did not specifically prohibit Indians from attending white schools; although, it did state that schools were open only to tax-paying landowners.[20] Because California had not recognized any formal Indian land rights, few California Indians were legally recognized as property owners. In 1860, the Common School Act was strengthened and actually excluded Indians along with Blacks and Asians.[21] In 1866, the law was altered to allow for admission of half-blood Indians and Indians residing with white families. Continuing in a policy that allowed gradual Indian integration, the California legislature passed an act in 1874 allowing Indians to attend separate schools if available. If such segregated facilities were not available, Indians were allowed to attend schools with the white children.[22]

With some exceptions, the state government, acting upon the wishes of the dominant Anglo society, repeatedly passed acts and regulations that aided in the discrimination — if not extermination of the Native American culture and of the natives themselves. Indenture, public humiliation, harsh punishment, inequity, and racism characterized various laws governing California Indians. In his thorough analysis of the legal status of California Indians, Chauncey S. Goodrich concluded: "The swift economic development of California was bought at a certain cost of human values. It was the Indian who paid the price."[23]

Chapter VI

Suffering for the Great Cause:
Years of Neglect, 1850-1865

With the American takeover of California, the United States government ostensibly assumed control of California's Indians immediately after statehood. In fact, the transition from a Mexican state to one of the American states left native peoples in limbo. Caught in the battle between states rights and federal policy, California Indians were trapped into a destiny not of their own making. The void of federal Indian policy in California is reflected in a letter from the commissioner of Indian affairs to California superintendent, Adam Johnson. In a revealing communication dated April 14, 1849, the commissioner wrote that little was known of the condition, population, or situation of native Californians. Thus, "no specific instructions relative to them can be given at the present."[1] The commissioner ordered Superintendent Johnson to count, scrutinize, and otherwise become knowledgeable of the various tribes so that future relations and treaties could be intelligently formulated.[2]

Following this inauspicious start, the early 1850s witnessed sporadic efforts on the part of the federal government to aid or placate, San Diego Native Americans. Following months of bureaucratic manipulations and policy changes, in late 1850, the federal government, acting through the Interior Department, appointed three Indian agents for California. Redick McKee, George W. Barbour, and Dr. Oliver M. Wozencraft received appointments as California's first agents. However, Congress failed to appropriate any money for the agents, which in effect placed their status and authority in jeopardy.[3] Side-stepping congressional processes, Interior Secretary A.H.H. Stuart suspended the three agents in late 1850, instead naming them as special treaty commissioners and awarding them a salary of $8.00 per day plus expenses.[4] Acting on these orders, McKee, Barbour, and Wozencraft left for California with ambiguous instructions that included the authority to negotiate with California's tribes and to make treaties. The three commissioners were not empowered to deal with or resolve land cessions. They could not establish Indian reservations and they had no funds to offer the natives.[5]

Realizing that they had very little to offer the Indians, the commissioners wrote to the commissioner of Indian affairs, Luke Lea, inquiring into the matter of Indian land rights and the possibility of setting aside lands for reservations. The letter was largely a moot and empty gesture. Without waiting for a reply, which never came, the men began signing treaties on March 19, 1851, without any authority to cede land or make monetary commitments. As the treaty commissioners worked their way south toward San Diego, California Native Americans grew impatient with the ineffective government officials regarding a proper settlement of land rights. While San Diego's Indians waited for the commissioners, the county sheriff illegally claimed jurisdiction over Indians, assessing them a tax on the same basis as their white neighbors. As a result, Indian lands fell prey to county officials when Native Americans failed to pay their taxes. Furthermore, the sheriff also failed to remove white squatters from Indian lands, thus allowing additional native lands to fall from local Indian control.

In San Diego, Sheriff Agoston Haraszthy decreed that although Indians lacked the rights of citizens, they possessed the obligations of citizens, including an obligation to pay local taxes. Addressing himself to this issue Haraszthy asserted that "There is no doubt that the possessions, real and personal, of Christianized Indians, are taxable."[6] The efforts to tax the Indians and the concomitant confiscation of land and property combined with a general feeling of anxiety led, in part, to the ill-fated Garra uprising of 1851. The Garra affair represented the first test of the federal government's position in southern California. Beginning in November 1851, while the treaty commissioners negotiated in central California and continuing until mid-January 1852, Cupenos and Luisenos under the leadership of Antonio Garra fought an unsuccessful battle to oust the Anglo intruders from their lands. Friendly Cahuilla and Northern Diegueno Indians sided with the whites as did most Luisenos, thus aiding the rapid conclusion of the so-called Garra Revolt. Garra and other Luiseno leaders were executed as was a chief of the Eastern Yumas. With the removal of the rebel leaders and the burning of several key villages "southern California returned to normal."[7]

In January 1852, Oliver M. Wozencraft, one of the three special treaty commissioners, arrived in San Diego County and concluded two treaties with local Indians.[8] On January 5, 1852, he completed the Treaty of Temecula with Luiseno and Cahuilla Indians of northern San Diego County. Two days later, Wozencraft concluded the Treaty of Santa Ysabel with Ipai and Tipai leaders.[9] At Temecula, Wozencraft sought reasons for Garra's recent revolt and tried to learn why otherwise peaceful Indians had started the armed conflict. Tribal leaders reported that the Indians had revolted for several reasons. Most importantly, the Indians had been pushed into the conflict by Haraszthy's unjust tax. In addition, the United States had failed to recognize Indian land rights, as guaranteed by General Stephen Watts Kearny. No matter how well intended, Kearny, of course, had no authority to make a promise to native peoples, but he was only one in a long line of military men who overstepped their commands and presented empty claims to local Indians. Finally, the Indian leaders reported that local Mexican leaders had convinced Garra and others that the only alternatives to revolt were slavery and death.[10] Already, a segment of Indian leadership had come to believe that the Americans were infidels and untrustworthy, feelings that Wozencraft and his successors would do little to assuage.

Wozencraft's two treaties initially held some promise. In general, he designed both treaties along the lines typical of the sixteen treaties previously completed by Wozencraft, Barbour, and McKee in California between 1851 and 1852. In each case, Indians ceded large land areas, securing for themselves a paltry number of acres. The Indians were also to receive educational aid and a supply of livestock and dry goods.[11] In most cases, small bands or even extended families were presumed to represent entire tribes, signing treaties that they were not authorized to sign, offered by commissioners not authorized to present the documents.[12] As one authority asserted: "Taken all together, one cannot imagine a more poorly conceived, more inaccurate, less informed, and less democratic process than the making of the eighteen treaties in 1851-1852 with the California Indians. It was a farce from the beginning to end."[13] And so began federal Indian policy in California.

When officials from the Indian Bureau presented the treaties to the United States Senate in the spring of 1852, they found virtually no support. Even those men who had hoped for some sort of honest effort on the part of the federal government disclaimed the eighteen treaties of McKee, Barbour, and Wozencraft.[14] Senators and representatives offered numerous and vociferous objections to the treaties. California representative Joseph W. McCorkle, a Democrat representing Sutter County, addressed the Senate and emotionally voiced the fears and anxieties of many white Californians. "The reservations of land which they (the commissioners) have set aside... comprise, in many cases," he suggested, "the most valuable agricultural and mineral land in the State."[15] McCorkle asserted that he did not endorse any part of the treaties and opposed the policy as a whole. Echoing McCorkle's fears, California Governor John Bigler addressed the California legislature on January 30, 1853, asking the legislators to urge the Senate to reject the treaties.[16] Acting on the suggestions of Governor Bigler and the findings of a special committee, Samuel Purdy, the president of the California Senate, reported on February 11, 1852, that messages were being forwarded "instructing our Senators and requesting our Representatives... to induce the Federal Government to remove the Indians of this State beyond its jurisdiction."[17] California's anwer to the Indian land rights problem was to pack the various tribes comprising tens of thousands of Indians off to the rapidly eroding Indian Territory.

Local land-hungry Anglos sought ways and means to remove the Indians from potentially productive land. The last thing they or their legislators desired was a rigid definition of Indian land ownership or boundaries. At a time when the Mexican Californios were fighting exhaustive legal battles to secure their own land titles, Native Americans had little chance to prove "legal" title to their lands when land title was based on ability to produce written documents. Voicing the general opinion of most of California's newspapers, the **Los Angeles Star** applauded the actions of the California legislature, warning that "to place upon our most fertile soil the most degraded race of Aboriginies upon the North American Continent...is planting the seeds of future disaster and ruin."[18] The result of such journalistic attacks, legislative protests, and political maneuvering was that the United States Senate rejected the treaties of 1852 without a lengthy debate. The treaties failed Senate ratification because of citizen protest, California legislature pressure, and the white fear that treaty lands might contain gold.[19]

Following Senate rejection of the treaties, anxious Indian Bureau officials placed Indian agents in charge of various tribes and invested them with the task of keeping the peace. In an effort to keep tight control over the agents and avoid any over-zealous action, the government imposed a federal policy of wait-and-see. In essence, the order of the day was much the same as it had been in 1849. Agents were to complete a census, observe the actions of the various tribes, and maintain friendly relations. The commissioner of Indian affairs ordered the agents to be as thrifty as possible. Funds became scarce, and so little money was available in 1852 that Wozencraft wrote to the commissioner of Indian affairs, complaining that he had to borrow money to pay his individual expenses while on government duty.[20] Even when Congress approved funds, federal agencies made rather strange appropriations. Noting that Congress had appropriated $100,000 for California Indians, the **Los Angeles Star** informed its readers that $25,000 worth of beads had just been received in California and that "the Superintendent is sorely puzzled what use to put them."[21] The government had promised livestock, educational aid, and dry goods, but instead California Indians received trade beads, hardly a life-sustaining commodity.

Lack of funds plagued various levels of Indian affairs during the era from 1850 to 1880. The effect was demoralizing to the few Indian agents who earnestly labored in vain to aid their wards. In February 1853, Indian agent, Benjamin D. Wilson appointed his close friend Judge Benjamin Hayes as temporary subagent for San Diego County. Wilson instructed Hayes to visit

Jose Manuel Hatam, respected Indian leader from a band inhabiting present-day Balboa Park, circa 1874. Courtesy Yuma County Historical Society.

villages in the district "and make such distributions among the Indians as in your judgment may be done with the limited means that I am prepared to give you for that purpose."[22] As far as can be ascertained, the efforts of Hayes and Wilson were the first earnest, albeit under-funded, attempt on the part of the federal government to alleviate the growing poverty and despair facing the dispossessed Indians in San Diego. For the most part, the federal and state governments were preoccupied with pacifying the Northern and Central Indians of California and establishing the costly and extensive Tejon Reservation just north of Los Angeles.

In 1853, Indian Superintendent Edward F. Beale began channeling money and effort into the Tejon Reservation in hopes that it would serve as a showcase and testimony of his efforts to "civilize" the California Indians. According to Beale's plan, government agents would force Indians to raise crops, manufacture goods, and raise cattle as part of an on-the-job training program which would enable them to become productive members of white society.[23] The reservation at Tejon would serve as an example for all other future reservations. Located in the extreme southern part of the San Joaquin Valley, Tejon served the Tule and Tejon Indians and became a source of anguish to San Diego County Indians, who increasingly felt slighted by the obvious manner in which funds and supplies were expended at Tejon. To San Diego Indians, it seemed as though the troublesome Indians of the north were receiving all that was promised in the treaties of 1852, while peaceful Indians suffered.

Realizing that local Indians needed more than vague promises and infrequent visits from Judge Hayes, Agent Wilson appointed a well-known local resident as subagent. In June 1853, Cave J. Couts, Sr., of San Luis Rey, became the first Indian subagent of San Diego County, replacing Benjamin Hayes. In a letter to Couts, agent Wilson outlined the goals of his program, warning Couts that the government did not have treaty plans or supplies for the Indians. Despite these limitations, Wilson told Couts to "protect the Indians in their rights, against impious white men. Settle all disputes amongst themselves; advise the Indians, encourage them to labor and provide for the maintenance of their families."[24]

As Couts began his tenure as agent, Superintendent Beale alienated many San Diego Native Americans by reappointing an unpopular and unrespected Indian alcalde. Beale's reappointment of the aged chieftan, Tomas, met with great disfavor among the Mesa Grande Indians. The Indians petitioned Couts to remove Tomas and replace him with the respected and dynamic Panto from San Pasqual. Tomas, who may have been verging on senility, lost a great deal of his people's respect when he was publicly flogged for stealing.[25] Couts responded to Indian demands in May 1854, removing Tomas and appointing Panto as the alcalde for the Mesa Grande region.

Although his actions were questioned by some local whites, Couts defended himself by pointing out that the well-being and content of the Indians were his main concern and that Indians were a federal not state or local problem.[26] The controversy surrounding Couts' action was soon forgotten, and he was later appointed permanent Indian subagent for San Diego County.

The conflict between the deposed Tomas and his successor, Panto, is noteworthy. In later years both Indian agents and superintendants followed a time-honored tradition of the Indian Bureau, undermining Indian self-determination by removing alcaldes whom they found personally displeasing and appointing Indians whom they favored. They did this, of course, without consulting tribal leaders. Although a degree of self-determination was allowable and advocated by Couts in 1854, it was a concept that fell upon hard times in the ensuing years. Couts, a federally appointed official, was an honorable man and served local Indians generally well, although he apparently physically abused some of his Indian workers. A letter to the **San Diego Herald** in 1855 suggested that Couts had been guilty of killing several Indians by using harsh and inhumane methods of punishment.[27] In January 1856, H.S. Burton, who was passing through the county on government business, noted that many persons knew of Couts' harsh discipline and considered him guilty of killing two Indians in July 1855, although he was never formally charged.[28]

In 1865, Couts was again accused of mistreating Indians, and Agent W.E. Lovett went to Couts' ranch to investigate the matter. Lovett reported that the La Jolla band of Indians thought highly of Couts. He reportedly had never interfered with their rights nor mistreated them. Lovett specifically denied that Couts was guilty of whipping an Indian boy to death, although he asked Couts to refrain from beating his Indian domestics.[29] In a recent study of Couts, a biographer defended him against the charges of whipping Indians to death and notes that even if this one case is valid, it remains an isolated blemish on an otherwise distinguished public record.[30] In 1854, Thomas J. Henley became superintendent of Indian affairs and reappointed Cave Couts as subagent for San Diego County. As was the case with his predecessor, Henley had few funds to offer the Indians. When he took over the post from Beale "the latter had only $1,260 to turn over to Henley."[31] The new superintendent wrote Couts in June 1855, ordering him to protect the Indians and keep the peace. He warned Couts that he was "not authorized to expend any money or contract any obligations in the discharge of your duties, for the present."[32] As would be the case with most of the California superintendents, Henley was dogged by chronic underfunding.

Couts immediately replied to Henley, stating that in spite of the costs, certain problems needed immediate attention if the government sincerely hoped to aid Indians and prevent violence between whites and Indians.[33] Couts suggested that the government establish a reservation system that would designate specific public property as Indian land, thus removing it from the land that settlers and squatters could preempt. Couts also suggested that the Indian Bureau select a single agent with the authority to appoint a single Indian alcalde to oversee the various rancherias and tribes. For his service, this alcalde would receive $30 to $40 per month and official recognition. Couts hoped that Manuelito Cota, a local Luiseno leader whose powers were significantly increased through white support, could fill such a position in reward for his previous faithful service to the United States. Couts further recommended that the Bureau of Indian Affairs provide him with between $2,000 and $3,000 to purchase agricultural implements and grains so local Indians could increase their farming. Couts also suggested that the War Department disengage itself from all Indian affairs and that one nonmilitary man be appointed Indian agent.[34] Couts provided thoughtful and reasonable solutions to pressing problems. He correctly identified land rights as a major point of disagreement and discontent among the local natives. His desire to appoint a single Indian alcalde was a typical frontier solution to Indian factionalism, but not one compatible with the political structure of the several independent and autonomous bands of southern California.

Couts' application for a single nonmilitary agent was a pragmatic appeal for a semi-permanent agent who could establish a rapport with Indians and at the same time be the only person responsible to the government. In the past, as Couts reported to Henley, it was not unusual for each and every ranking military man who passed through the area to assert his authority over the Indians and attempt to intimidate them with his military might. Couts' request for funds to purchase items for agricultural development was reasonable and one that followed the stated goals of the Indian office. It had earlier been realized that the Indians of San Diego County were carrying out various levels of agriculture and that with a minimal amount of assistance they could become totally self-sufficient, even in the face of continued loss of land and water rights. Superintendent Henley evidently considered the subagent's suggestions but failed to act upon them. In August 1857, one year after Couts made his suggestions, Henley received yet another set of requests from San Diego. Major George Blake, the commandant of the military post at San Diego, requested $5,000 worth of supplies for those San Diego Indians to the south and beyond Couts' immediate jurisdiction. Henley, who had never been south of the Tejon Reservation in his three years in office, refused Blake's request to help feed the Indians.[35]

Judge Hayes and others, including local newspapers, were aware of

Henley's seeming disregard for Indians living in San Diego County. In an editorial, backing the reappointment of Cave Couts, the **San Diego Herald** lashed out at Henley, calling him a useless politico and suggesting his removal.[36] In April 1859, Henley was relieved of his duties based on a charge of misappropriation of funds for allegedly using Indian laborers to construct a private mill on a government reserve. He was also accused of using government funds to purchase supplies for the mill and loaning out supplies earmarked for Indians to white laborers who worked on the mill.[37] Although Henley may have been a poor administrator, his ineptness was not unique. The California Indian superintendency was plagued by a variety of problems. Paramount among these problems was the procrastination of Indian agents in ordering supplies, general administrative ineptitude and inexperience on the part of agents, a past record of bad credit, the lack of communication between the California superintendent and Washington, and graft.[38] The various California superintendents were not able to pay their own employees, or establish a means of distributing the available goods, let alone make or implement policies that would actually aid the Indians.

Amid the financial turmoil and mismanagement, H.S. Burton visited the Indians of San Diego County in January 1856, to evaluate their condition and attitudes for a detailed federal report. On January 17 at San Bernardo, a rancheria near present-day Rancho Bernardo, Burton talked with Panto, captain of the San Pasqual Indians and alcalde for the Ipai people, who urgently requested "protection from our government against the encroachments of squatters upon the lands legally granted to his people."[39] Burton investigated Panto's accusations, discovering that five or six white squatters were taking up the best Indian land. Burton suggested in his report that "this is a just and proper occasion for the personal interference of the superintendent of Indian affairs."[40] Continuing his inquiry, Burton met with Manual Cota who, upon the death in 1855 of Chief Pablo Apis and with Couts' backing, assumed control over most of the major northern Luiseno villages, including Pauma, Potrero, and Temecula. Burton learned that Cota was highly displeased with the multiplicity of Indian agents and subagents. The headman stated that every government agent or military officer who entered the area warned him against listening to, or following, orders from any other governmental official. As leader of his people who was he to believe, he inquired. Addressing himself to the inaction of Superintendent Henley, Cota brought up the frequently expressed sentiment that the government was concerned only with the northern Indians and chose to ignore the friendly Indians of San Diego County. "Why does he not come to see us as well as the Indians of the Tulare and the Indians of the north," the irate chief spoke harshly of Superintendent Henley, stating that his people were entitled to land and supplies and that "we claim his attention as much as they do."[41] Burton agreed but offered no resolution.

In June 1856, Burton met with Chief Tomas of San Pasqual to inquire how conditions were among the Ipai. Tomas told Burton that he had witnessed a terrible deterioration of his people and expressed a feeling of hopelessness. Tomas echoed Panto's and Manual Cota's concern that the warlike northern Indians received great quantities of aid while the peaceful Indians of San Diego starved as a result of the gradual influx of Anglos upon their ancient homeland.[42] Remembering the treaties of 1852 that he had signed, Tomas asked Burton what had become of the promises of Commissioner Wozencraft. Burton replied that the United States government would not honor the treaties or the promises made in council. Burton's lengthy report on his field trip was sympathetic to the Indians' plight, and his suggestion that the superintendent should act was valid, perhaps raising the spirit and morale of the disenchanted Indians, at least temporarily. However, Burton's efforts failed. Within ten years, Tomas and the San Pasqual Indians were forced by local officials to abandon their ancestral lands and leave the bones of their dead for the white man's plow. The Mesa Grande band, under Panto, was further harassed and increasingly lost land to white squatters. These leaders and their people were never officially informed that the treaty they had signed in good faith in 1852 had been rejected and locked away in a cold steel government safe.

As the 1850s drew to a close, the commissioner of Indian affairs admitted that the previous ten years of effort had been less than successful and that "management of our Indian Affairs in California has been embarrassed with a great variety of difficulties. Neither the government of the United States nor the State of California recognizes in the Indians any right of exclusive occupancy to any specific lands."[43] In a period characterized by a steady influx of white settlers into southern California, the federal government was unwilling, or at best unable, to formulate, let alone enforce, a consistent Indian policy that would guarantee Native American land rights. J. Ross Browne, a special agent assigned to assess the condition of California's Indians, lamented the loss of Indian lands. He quipped that the notion, "strange as it may appear, never occurred to them the Indians that they were suffering for the great cause of civilization, which, in the natural course of things, must exterminate Indians."[44]

As a new decade dawned, President Abraham Lincoln struggled to develop an Indian policy in which the federal government would make increased overtures toward Native Americans. With the outbreak of the Civil War, government priorities turned toward crushing the southern insurrection. The annual report of the commissioner of Indian affairs for 1861 noted that as a result of the war, John P.H. Wentworth, California Indian affairs

Luiseno Indian woman from Pala. Courtesy San Diego Historical Society.

commissioner, lacked the funds to visit the tribes of San Bernardino and San Diego. The report stated that a cutoff of money might seriously impair the possibility of keeping the Indians contented and peaceful.[45] In his annual report for 1865, Special Agent W.E. Lovett examined the effects of the Civil War on Native Americans of San Diego County. He rationalized that although they were nearly forgotten, "the civil war...is a sufficient excuse for this apparent neglect."[46] During the Civil War, state and federal officials feared that the Indians of San Diego would follow the lead of other tribes and not remain loyal to the Union. Such fears were, to a large degree, based on the activities of some dispossessed Indian groups in the Indian Territory and the old Southwest who saw the Civil War as a chance to either escape from the burden of the white man or to side with the Southerners in the hope that they would later be afforded better treatment than they had previously received at the hands of federal agents.[47] To ensure that secessionists and Southern sympathizers were kept on the defensive, Ramon Carrillo, an influential rancher near Temecula, convinced a group of Cahuilla warriors to roam the adjacent mountains in search of insurgents.[48] Indians in southern California remained quiet throughout the war, maintaining their loyalty to the United States government. Indeed, when the Civil War started, Indians living in San Diego County cut a liberty pole and hoisted the Stars and Stripes to its top to display their patriotism. Addressing the problem of rebel activities among the Indians, the **Wilmington Journal** noted: "It is astonishing that these tribes have behaved so well considering the pernicious teachings they have received from vile secessionists in their midst."[49]

Unlike other regions in the West, San Diego County did not witness any Indian uprisings or armed conflict during the Civil War, although Anglo anxieties heightened whenever Indians sporadically asserted their rights to lands and sought to maintain their livelihood by whatever means open to them, including theft. Agent Couts wrote to Ephraim Morse in 1864 that Francisco, general of the Luiseno, was causing trouble over property rights and should be removed from his position.[50] A year later, Agent Lovett reported that Francisco had resigned from his chieftainship and that Manual Cota had been appointed. Perhaps Couts, through Morse, had persuaded officials that Francisco was unsuitable.[51] Although Lovett used the word "resigned" regarding Francisco's actions, the **Wilmington Journal** indicated that he had been removed.[52]

The months immediately following the Civil War were devoted to the reconstruction of the South, developing a foreign policy, and reassuring the Indians of the Indian Territory and the Great Plains that the United States had their best interests at heart. In southern California, little was done to appease or help the troubled Native Americans. The government provided some badly needed aid in the spring of 1865. Realizing that the drought of 1864-1865 had wiped out the usually productive farms of the Indians, Agent John Q.A. Stanley, requested that the government furnish plows and seeds for those rancherias most in need. In his request, Stanley lamented that Indians were being sold cheap whiskey by Mexicans who in turn induced the Indians to steal in order to purchase more liquor. Stanley stressed that the past season had been severe for the Indians and that some were migrating to white settlements where they were forced to beg for a meager living.[53] Upon receipt of Stanley's urgent letter, superintendent of Indian affairs, Austin Wiley acted promptly, forwarding twelve plows, twelve plow harnesses, twelve dozen hoes, twenty pounds of melon seed, and thirty pounds of pumpkin seed.[54] Since corn and beans cost less in Los Angeles than at the bureau headquarters at San Francisco, Wiley requested that Stanley purchase those seeds in Los Angeles.

By April 18, 1865, Agent Stanley was in the field distributing a portion of the goods to Luiseno villages near San Luis Rey. On May 1, he arrived at Pala to assess the condition of Indians assembled there. Stanley found the Indians generally satisfied but still disgruntled over the recent removal of Chief Francisco and the reappointment of Manual Cota.[55] Following the meeting at Pala, Stanley traveled to Temecula and called a general council of all Indians from the surrounding area. According to Stanley, eight or ten Luiseno captains met at Temecula along with 100 Cahuillas led by Manuel Largo. On May 5, a party of over 100 Ipai and Tipai led by the aged Tomas, arrived at Temecula. By May 8, Stanley had completed the distribution of goods, thus marking the first time that the government had made a large-scale contribution to the welfare of the Indians of San Diego.

The villages represented at Temecula included Potrero, Agua Grande, San Ygnacio, Temecula, San Luis Rey, Coyotes, Santa Rosa, La Jolla, Saboba, Pala, Pauma, Chola, San Ysidro, Agua Caliente, La Puerta de la Cruz, and Puerta Chiquita. Lovett stated that ten Ipai and Tipai leaders could not attend the meeting because of the great distance and recommended that these men assemble for a future conference.[56] Despite the absence of these leaders, the government convened a successful council. Lovett reported that over 1400 Indians attended the meeting at Temecula and that they brought with them a census of their population and accounts of their livestock and produce, marked by cuts in long strips of wood. Besides receiving goods, families came forth and presented their grievances. Although the majority of the complaints were described as minor, Lovett noted that some, involving land rights, were serious. Cahuillas from San Timoteo complained that during the smallpox epidemic of 1862-1863, they fled from their lands to escape the disease. In their absence, nearby whites moved on to Indian land, claiming possession and forcing the Cahuillas to lead more nomadic lives.

The theft of land also encourages the Indians to commit depredation against whites. The Luisenos at Pejamo, a seasonal village near Temecula, faced a similar problem. When the Indians left the village for their summer foraging rounds, local whites, led by men named Breeze and Wolfe, entered the village, set fire to Indian homes, and took possession of the land and the nearby water supply. Lovett suggested to the commissioner of Indian affairs that whites involved in the San Timoteo and Pejamo affairs be punished and that the land be restored to its rightful owners. Unfortunately, no action was taken and the land never was returned to the Indians.[57]

The needs of the San Diego County Indians, Lovett said, were few, although prompt assistance was needed. Specifically, he recommended that clothing, seeds, and agricultural implements be provided; that liquor traders be driven off; and that mission churches be restored as a means of ensuring the spiritual welfare of the Indians. Except for recommendations on the San Timoteo and Pejamo affair, Lovett officially ignored the problem of land rights and white squatters, not wishing to confront the volatile issue facing the region. The federal government refused to stop white squatters from settling on Indian land and failed to control whites who were manipulating Native Americans for their own personal gain. As was the case in many Indian communities in the American West, a whole body of devious and shrewd Indian traders settled on or near the Indian rancherias and began their sordid business. Although Indian traders had been in San Diego since the late 1830s, the liquor trade was booming by the mid-1860s. Superintendent B.C. Whiting reported the problem: "These invaders are selling liquor to the Indians and trading with them. They have already got away with most of their oxen and cattle, horses, grains, beans and other property.... There are but a few of them who have teams left with which to cultivate the ground and put in a crop for ensuing years."[58]

The do-nothing policy of the federal government was advocated and appreciated by most white land owners, local newspaper editors, and would-be land owners. Government Indian policy, at least in part, was shaped by public opinion, political representatives, and newspapers, reflecting their readers' views. As Native Americans protested the loss of their lands, Anglos in southern California increased their agitation for control over all available lands, including those claimed by Indians. To some Anglos, the rapidly decreasing Indian population was positive, desirable, and beneficial to American expansion. Some whites believed that God was clearing the path for his chosen people to ensure the Manifest Destiny of the United States. The **San Francisco Alta** reported that since 1851, over 22,000 California Indians had died and that they "had abandoned their habits of regular industry, and began to die off rapidly...most of the survivors are living away from the whites in a condition little superior to savagism."[59] Yet the **Alta** boasted that since the signing of the Treaty of Guadalupe Hidalgo, ending the Mexican War in 1848 and bringing California under American control, "we have no reason, as Americans, to be ashamed of work which we have done in California."[60] Evidently the editors saw no meaningful correlation between Manifest Destiny in California and the death of 22,000 native Californians.

In the fifteen years between statehood and the end of the Civil War, Native Americans in San Diego were given a low priority and relegated to suffering with a set of ambiguous, unevenly applied and seriously underfunded Indian policies.[61] Federal Indian policy during the era from 1850 to 1865 was characterized by five years of near-total ignorance and faltering tokenism. During the Civil War, the Indian Bureau largely ignored Indian policy, making the Indians of San Diego County fair game for land hungry, self-centered whites who illegally expropriated hundreds of acres of Indian lands that were never returned to the Indian people. At a time when reservations were being established throughout the country and some genuine efforts were being made to consolidate Indian lands, Indians throughout San Diego County were ignored and neglected. The harvest of unevenly dictated and applied Indian policies was that the Indian people were largely ignored at a time when their very existence was threatened. Although the neglect may be considered, in some cases, benign, the end result was, nevertheless, painfully real.

Chapter VII

Toward a Reservation System 1865-1874

Beginning with California statehood in 1850 and continuing through post Civil War reconstruction, the letters, annual reports, and messages of various Indian agents, superintendents, and commissioners were filled with recommendations and plans for establishing Indian reservations in San Diego County. Plans for reservations and monies to finance them fell upon the deaf ears of congressional leaders who seemed more intent on pumping money into the military containment of Indians or into the larger reservations in northern California. Realization that Indians needed established and protected tracts of land can be traced back, at least as early as the 1850s, when Indian Agent Adam Johnston suggested that parcels of land be permanently assigned to the Mission Indians. Two years later, in 1852, Cave J. Couts made the first formal request for a reservation. He suggested to Superintendent Beale that the Ipai and Luisenos of San Diego County would prosper and burden the government less if placed on a reservation.[1]

Agitation for reservations in San Diego increased in 1856 following a bad year for Indian crops and a shortage of edible wild plants, such as mesquite and acorns. In a letter to Superintendent Henley, dated July 7, 1856, Couts again suggested the government establish a suitable reservation for Indians under his jurisdiction.[2] That same year, the influential **Los Angeles Star** fell short of actually advocating a reservation system, but did recommend that cattle, blankets, and other supplies be provided for the Indians to ease their misery, resulting from a horrible drought.[3] By the fall of 1858 the **Star** concluded that the only way to provide properly for San Diego's Indians was to establish a reservation system, ensuring that Indians were provided with the basic necessities of life. The motives of the **Los Angeles Star** were hardly altruistic and not based on a desire to aid the Indians. The editor of the **Star** stated that a reservation would provide protection and security for the Indians, but, more important, a reservation would protect local whites, a necessity to encourage white immigration to southern California.[4]

Between 1865 and 1870, reports from Indian agents in San Diego as well as from commissioners of Indian affairs presented an ambiguous picture of the land holdings and conditions among local Indians. In 1866, Agent Stanley wrote that the supplies provided to Indians the previous year were well-received and put to good use. Furthermore, he stated that had it not been for the damning effects of local rumsellers and outlaws, the Indians would have been quite comfortable.[5] Stanley's report suggested, as did most reports from 1860 to 1870, that a reservation was badly needed to ensure that the farming activities of the Indians continued and to separate Indians from undesirable whites who lived on the fringes of native settlements.

During January 1867, Stanley made another distribution of goods to Indians, including those at Agua Caliente. Using that village as a temporary headquarters, Stanley sent runners to various Indian villages to inform the people to come to Agua Caliente to receive their portion of the goods.[6] Because of the absence of several chiefs and the distance that they had to travel, Stanley completed the distribution on February 6, 1867. He noted that because large numbers of Indians sought goods, he was forced to distribute only a small portion to captains from twelve villages who attended the meeting. He instructed them to divide the goods among the most needy and reminded them that the tools were to be shared in common. Articles distributed included calico, hoes, blankets, and seeds.

Returning from Agua Caliente, Stanley made arrangements to distribute goods and tools to other Luisenos and Ipai. A meeting was called at Puerta Cruz for February 18, but bad weather and difficult traveling prevented the widely dispersed Indian captains from arriving at the village until February 20. Once assembled, at least twenty village leaders met with Stanley.[7] He divided the goods into twenty equal parts and provided enough implements to encourage each village to continue its agricultural pursuits. Following the distribution, Stanley called the chiefs together and lectured them regarding the advantages of constructing better dwellings, planting fruit trees, and generally establishing permanent homes.

Ironically, although Stanley advocated establishing permanent homes and tending the land, he could not guarantee that the Indians' land rights would be respected. In essence, Stanly asked Indians to make improvements on the land which, once enhanced, would or could be legally preempted by a white person. Stanley admitted to California superintendent of Indian affairs, B.D. Whiting, that in spite of Stanley's personal cajoling and promises, it was evident that "the whites are pushing back on the frontier, and unless lands are reserved for the use of the Indians, soon they will have no place to live."[8]

Stanley was not alone in his pessimism regarding San Diego County Indians. In his annual report of 1867, Reverend N.G. Taylor, the commissioner of Indian affairs, lamented that numerous previous annual reports had

Samuel Curo, Ipai-Tipai, holding golden eagle for ceremony, 1907. Courtesy Museum of the American Indian.

clearly documented the needs of the Indians but nothing had been done for them. Hoping to ensure that some form of aid was given to Native Americans, Taylor strongly suggested that a suitable tract of land be set aside for them and a special investigator be assigned to their district to assess needs and report back to the government.[9] Consequently, another investigator was sent to San Diego County and a report was filed, yet no attempts at establishing a reservation were made. Taylor's recommendations joined those of Stanley, Couts, and Johnston in the bulging filing cabinets gracing the Office of Indian Affairs. Having been propelled from a prehistoric hunting and gathering economy into an industrial-agricultural system, Indians became increasingly cut off from traditional means of support. Denied basic land rights, they were still unable to participate in the dominant economy.

In his annual report of 1868 to Commissioner Taylor, Superintendent Whiting expressed his bitter disappointment with Congress for not acting on numerous department recommendations to establish a San Diego reservation and wrote that he had "cherished the hope that some appropriations would be made by the late session of Congress to enable me to establish a reservation for the Mission Indians."[10] Whiting's suggestion that San Pasqual and Pala Valleys be surveyed and set aside as reservations went unheeded. In 1868, he implored the commissioner of Indian affairs to act with haste to secure lands for the increasingly desperate Indians. In a letter to Commissioner Taylor, Whiting stated that available, arable land in San Diego was rapidly being settled and that Indians were steadily being pushed from their homelands. In a note of quiet, bureaucratic desperation, Whiting concluded the letter by observing that "immediate steps will be absolutely necessary to protect the Indians in their rights and to protect the interference of the whites."[11]

In 1869, politically devisive impeachment proceedings against President Andrew Johnson and severe economic instability thwarted Commissioner Taylor's efforts to be a peacemaker.[12] In a reorganization of the Indian Affairs Office, both Whiting and Taylor were replaced. A staunch advocate of establishing large reservations, Taylor's policies bore little fruit in a time of such turmoil. His two-year tenure set the stage for later reforms, commonly called Grant's "Peace Policy," but Taylor left office a broken and disappointed man. Shortly after assuming office in March 1869, President Ulysses S. Grant and his advisors formulated and implemented his Indian Peace Policy. Grant sincerely believed that the Indians held a natural title to the land and that, to the Indians' detriment, the military had dominated past Indian policies. Over the next several years, Grant instituted several reforms. Notable among them included establishing a Board of Indian Commissioners to disburse funds and establish reservations and placing many

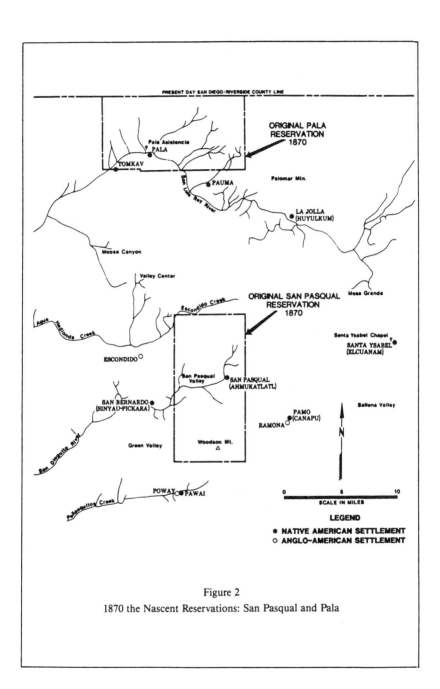

Figure 2
1870 the Nascent Reservations: San Pasqual and Pala

of the Indian agencies in the hands of Quakers. Much of the patronage that had led to the spoils system inherent in 19th century Indian affairs was thereby eliminated and military power in Indian affairs lessened.[13]

The results of Grant's Peace Policy and the earlier efforts of N.G. Taylor began rapidly to affect Indian policy in California. In a strongly worded letter to secretary of the interior, J.D. Cox, newly appointed commissioner of Indian affairs, E.S. Parker, a full-blooded Seneca, reported that the deplorable condition and extensive needs of the Mission Indians had been consistently reported with negligible results long enough.[14] Congress, Parker said, must now act to ensure that these Indians were guaranteed some property rights and basic assistance. Parker concluded his communication by stating that Superintendent John B. McIntosh was currently assessing land in San Diego for a reservation and believed that most of the Indians of the area would settle on such a reserve if one was established.

Superintendent McIntosh found that land was available in the Pala-San Pasqual region and that a reservation could be successfully established. McIntosh estimated that a total appropriation of $28,160 would be necessary to establish the reservation, including $15,000 for cattle, clothing, food, teams of animals, and farming implements. Realizing that Indians would need training, education, and medical attention, McIntosh also requested funds for a physician, a blacksmith, a miller, an agent, two teachers, and two farmers.[15]

After almost twenty years of effort, the government approved two reservations for San Diego County. President Grant set aside portions of Pala and San Pasqual Valleys by an executive order, signed January 31, 1870.[16] The land set aside for the San Pasqual Indians comprised Townships 12 and 13 south and Ranges 1 east and 1 west of the San Bernardino Meridian. The nascent reservation encompassed over 92,000 acres and included Ramona to the east, Mount Woodson to the south, Highland Valley on the west and Lake Wohlford to the north (Figure 2). The Pala Reserve comprised Township 9 south, Ranges 1 and 2 west of the San Bernardino Meridian. This reservation included about 46,000 acres situated between Palomar Mountain on the east, Pala Mountain on the south, Rice Canyon on the west, and the second standard parallel on the north.

An Indian agency was established at San Pasqual, headed by Indian Agent and former First Lieutenant Augustus P. Greene. Shortly after his appointment, Greene posted official signs and made public announcements identifying designated lands in the valleys as the acreage for future Indian reservations. The announcements read:

> Therefore all persons are hereby forbidden to make any improvements, and warned to make immediate preparations for

removing from these lands, and all persons are forbidden to settle in the respective Townships, indicated as reserved for Indian
purpose.[17]

Anglo response to the establishment of Indian reservations on arable land
was immediate and vociferous. Upon learning of the reservations, several
irate settlers hired a local lawyer, Charles P. Taggart, who until January
1870, was part owner of the influential **San Diego Union**, to present their
case in opposition to the reservation plan. A condition of the contract with
Taggart included a cash payment of $500 if he successfully had the order
establishing the reservations revoked.[18]

One of Taggart's first deeds was to publish inflammatory anti-reservation
material in the **San Diego Union**. On March 10, 1870, an editorial stated
that the government's plan for a reservation was a terrible idea, a swindle,
and a needless attempt to give valuable land to Indians who either already
had land or worked for local ranchers, living comfortably there. The
newspaper vowed to fight the reservation plan until it was rescinded.[19] By
April 1870, the **San Diego Union** had become a vehement critic of the reservation system and, indirectly, of Grant's Peace Policy. The **Union** claimed
that the whole reservation plan was a devious land scheme of McIntosh
and Greene who in turn were being funded by an alleged "Indian Ring"
in San Francisco.[20] The paper claimed that an anti-reservation petition
with 500 signatures had gone to Washington and that placing a reservation
on such fertile land would ruin the honest and hardworking people of San
Diego County. To substantiate its claims in opposition to the plan, the **San
Diego Union** asserted that the Indians did not need any more land because
they were content with their village garden plots. The **San Francisco Alta**,
on the other hand, maintained that the Indians deserved government protection from treacherous whites.[21]

While local whites and federal officials fought over implementation of
the reservation plan, Indians, the people hoping to benefit from such a plan,
remained in a state of confusion. Local anti-reservation whites told the Indians that if they moved onto the reservations they "were to be made slaves
of the Government; small-pox was to be introduced in the clothing sent
them; their cattle taken from them."[22] The ploy worked. Coupled with
reluctance to move to nontraditional tracts of land, white intimidation, and
faltering leadership among the white-appointed Indian leaders, the two
reservations remained unoccupied.

At the same time, a long standing feud between Manual Cota and
Olegario, both aspirants to the position of leader for all Luisenos, flared
up again, fueled in part by the planned reservations. Agent W.E. Lovett
had earlier reappointed Manuel Cota as the "general" or chief of the Lui-

seno Indians as once requested by Cave Couts.[23] Cota's original source of power, beyond that of village chief, can be traced back to September 1853, when Couts appointed him as captain general over a number of Luiseno, Cupeno, and Cahuilla villages.[24] Ineffectual in his dealings with non-Indians and unwise to their devious ways, Cota was well liked by whites, including officials of the Bureau of Indian Affairs. His tendency to compromise and capitulate seemed well suited to bureaucrats who abhorred troublesome Indians who asserted that they had rights. As Manuel Cota abused his people and steadily urged their removal to reservations, important Indian clan leaders acted. In late May 1870, leaders of numerous northern San Diego County villages supported Cota's ouster and replaced him with Olegario, an admired and respected Luiseno. Olegario, a traditional **net** or clan leader, understood the white world from his years of labor for influential Americans in and around Los Angeles.[25]

Realizing that Indian agents and other officials might disapprove of Olegario's chiefship, eleven village chiefs headed by Olegario traveled to the San Diego office of Judge Benjamin Hayes, seeking official certification of their decision to dispose of Cota and appoint Olegario.[26] Assuming that Cota and his white backers would seek to reinstate Cota and portray Olegario as an unsupported usurper, the disgruntled chiefs hoped to use white methods of certification through the written word which seemed to be so important to white officials. The **San Diego Union** of July 7, 1870, noted that on the first of the month, County Judge Thomas H. Bush, acting in concert with Judge Benjamin D. Hayes, certified a document in which Indian leaders declared their allegiance to Olegario. Chiefs from Pala, Agua Caliente, La-pichi, Aguanga, La Puerta, Chiquita, Puerta de la Cruz, Temecula, Vallecito, Pawii, San Ysidro, Potrero, and La Jolla swore that Olegario's appointment was the will of the Indian people:

> The people have elected for General Olegario Sali; and with said Captains, forty Indians in number make such declaration. At their request, I certify to this fact, for such action as may be judged proper by the Government.[27]

Judge Bush noted that as a group, leaders who signed the certification represented the most powerful and respected men from three different cultures and from geographically disparate villages. That they would band together and travel to San Diego revealed a solidarity of thought and action, previously lacking among these peoples, and indicated the low esteem in which they held Cota. The actual document attesting to Olegario's election had been written by Judge Hayes upon a complaint from Manuel Cota that Olegario was claiming power which Cota had previously held. Knowing of the complaint, Olegario and his followers sought to establish the fact that Cota did not represent the Indian people and that his accusations against Olegario were invalid. Aware of the controversial nature of certifying an Indian chief who was not government approved, both Hayes and Bush made it clear that they had merely certified a document inspired and drafted by the various Indian leaders.[28]

Judge Hayes later wrote that the Indian chiefs had adamantly stressed the need for an official document and that they "could not be satisfied, without this certificate of their acts — apparent by election."[29] Hayes also wrote that a primary motive for appointing Olegario and having the act certified was to gain aid from the government regarding their land rights. Fearful that Cota was pushing them into an ill-advised and ambiguous reservation system, Native American leaders "commenced taking steps for the management of their own affairs discarding Manuelito, who was considered to be a 'Reservationist' so to speak."[30]

Although Manuel Cota accused Olegario of blocking efforts of both the government and Cota to settle the San Pasqual Reservation issue, the concern of Olegario and his followers was justified. The official government papers establishing the reservation had not been received and Lieutenant Greene, the appointed reservation agent, feared for his life and the lives of his reluctant wards. Olegario correctly perceived that if his people moved to the reservation and deserted their traditional homelands, they would not be allowed to reclaim their ancestral lands, if the reservation tract was later taken away or otherwise compromised. Agent McIntosh quoted Cota as stating that Olegario had told his people not to "localize until the paper sent above has been heard from [referring probably to a paper sent to Washington to get the reservation order set aside]."[31]

Aware of the governmental betrayal of the California treaties of 1852, the ever shrinking lands in the Indian Territory, and the recent harsh dealings with the Indians in northern California, including the Modoc massacre and forced removals, Olegario remained adamant in his demands for protection of his people's land rights. Olegario and his sub-chiefs repeatedly visited officials both in San Diego and at San Pasqual in their attempts to obtain a valid certification of land title. Their efforts failed. On February 13, 1871, Commissioner of Indian Affairs Parker recommended to the secretary of the interior that the Pala and San Pasqual Reservation orders be revoked because:

> It appears...that the citizens of San Diego County protest against the order of the President setting aside said lands for Indian reservation; that the Indians are unanimously opposed to going on said reservation; that citizens have made valuable improvements thereon; and that there are but few Indians on

the land set apart as foresaid . . . and that the **opinion of the press,** together with other evidence, would indicate that it would be to the best interests and welfare of the Indians, as well as others, that . . . the order of the President . . . should be rescinded." [Emphasis added.][32]

Four days later, President Grant revoked his own executive order, returning over 69,000 acres to the public domain without any assurances that the Indians would ever receive title to one single acre.[33] Olegario's worst fears were confirmed; the rumors, protests, and threats of Taggart and others had prevailed. Had Olegario's people moved to the reservation as Cota had insisted, they would have been landless indigents without even the tenuous claim that they now possessed.

Throughout early 1871 and continuing into the summer months, animosity between Olegario and Cota increased to such a degree that white officials feared open tribal war. As a deposed supporter of a reservation plan that never reached fruition, Cota was hardly in an enviable position. Special Agent Augustus Greene reported in February 1871, that Manuel Cota feared for his life and was "virtually a prisoner in Pala."[34] Cota's sister, Margarita, was captured by Olegario's warriors and hung by her wrists until sympathetic elders forced her release. Realizing that Indians were frustrated in their attempts to settle the land problem and that the year of devastating drought had produced tremendous hardship, local Anglos feared the worst from the uncompromising Olegario. With memories of the Garra uprising only a generation removed, and the Great Plains about to erupt into Indian wars, Anglos worried that Olegario and his people might attempt to recover, by brute force, what was once theirs. During late August and the first week of September 1871, southern California newspapers repeatedly carried unsubstantiated articles that indicated an Indian uprising was imminent. Stirred into dread fear and anticipating violence, white residents of San Luis Rey and adjacent areas made preparations for evacuation and military confrontation.[35] The over-reaction and fears of local whites, whatever the basis, revealed the potential power that the Indians held over the sparsely-populated, non-Indian communities.

Once the rumor of Indian revolts had proven false and the fever pitch subsided, California Indian Affairs Superintendent B.C. Whiting, recently reappointed and a strong proponent of the reservation system and Grant's Peace Policy, decided to void the election of Olegario and appoint a chief of his choice. Ignoring the fact that Cota had already been deposed by his own people, Whiting requested and received Cota's resignation as general of the Luiseno Indians. To dispense with Olegario, Whiting simply stated that the election that brought Olegario to power was not official. Hoping that a compromise candidate would placate the Indians, Whiting appointed Jose Antonio Sal, a relative of Cota's, as general-in-chief.[36]

At least one local resident thought that persistent rumors of Indian revolt were scare tactics designed to discredit Olegario. Writing from San Pasqual, John Thompson, an influential rancher, informed the **San Diego Union**, in a letter dated September 10, 1871, that for years Manuel Cota had been the friend of the large land owners in the area to the detriment of his own people and that, "For this conduct and for other doings against the wishes and best interests of the tribes, they **deposed** him, and elected Olegario in his stead."[37] Thompson accused the **San Diego Union**, white officials, and agents of Cota of spreading false rumors of an Indian uprising in an attempt to disparage Olegario and undermine the Indians' efforts at liberty and self-determination. Thompson closed his letter to the newspaper suggesting that Indians be allowed to run their own affairs as recommended by Senator Charles Sumner before a recent congressional hearing, that the ouster of Manuel Cota was justified, and that the government should stop its token assistance. Instead, he asserted, the government should affirm land for Indians and provide them with plows instead of offering them blankets and food. Concluding, Thompson called Manuel Cota a tool of white reservationists.

A month after the **San Diego Union** printed Thompson's letter, the editor had a chance to meet Olegario in person. Feeling that he had been maligned by the press and that local whites did not understand his efforts, Olegario consented to an interview. The Indian chief, described as "very stout, rather tall, erect in bearing, and has a good natured and intelligent countenance" met with the press.[38] In this interview, Olegario informed the editor that a majority of Luisenos despised Manuel Cota and that Agent Lovett and Superintendent Whiting made serious mistakes by appointing Cota or one of his followers as general. Olegario claimed that Cota was not even a member of the tribe nor did he speak the same language. The Indian leader's view of the recent appointment of Jose Antonio Sal was that Whiting had called an election hoping that Cota would win. When the tribe rejected Cota again, Whiting appointed Jose Antonio.

As the year 1871 closed, a great deal of tension wound its way through the Anglo and Indian communities. As Whiting continued his support of Jose Antonio Sal, Olegario's supporters voiced their disapproval, believing that the loss of proposed reservation land and the government's effort to defeat their attempt at self-determination were clear indications of the ill-will and negative attitude of whites. Local Anglos thought that the government was ineffectual in its dealings with the Indians and unable to guarantee white safety. In a letter to Superintendent Whiting, a number of local ranchers and influential men voiced their disapproval of Olegario

Indian woman making beautiful and useful basket, circa 1880. Courtesy Yuma County Historical Society.

and their preference for Cota. The petition to Whiting included signatures of Louis Rose, Marcus Schiller, Andrew Cassiday, Benjamin Hayes, J.B. Bandini, Father Ubach, and other prominent persons. The petition alleged that the ouster of Cota, which they noted as "improper interference," had led to disorder, confusion, and lack of proper control over the Indians.[39] The petition further stated that Cota was honest, experienced, and active, asserting that the need for his continuance of office was crucial if the land and property rights of whites were to be maintained.

By March 1872, it was apparent that the chieftainship problem for the Luisenos was far from resolved. Jose Antonio sought officially to rebuke Olegario by lodging a complaint against him, claiming that he resisted the government sanctioned authority vested in Antonio.[40] Justice Locke studied the complaint which included the charge that Olegario was inciting his followers to ignore the government's edict appointing Jose Antonio. The local judge quite correctly declared that he had no authority to preside over an Indian matter of this type. The inability of either the federal or local government to settle the leadership dispute successfully caused continued anxieties among whites and Indians alike. Government authorities and knowledgeable whites knew that although Jose Antonio remained the white-appointed chief, he was merely an ineffective figurehead who did not represent or actually rule over his people. Olegario continued to be the actual chief of the Luisenos, albeit somewhat tacitly and removed from the public eye.

In June 1873, Olegario and ten Indian captains from the Pala region traveled to Los Angeles to visit Special Indian Agent John G. Ames. The captains presented Ames with a list of grievances that included: (1) loss of Indian land; (2) loss of water rights; (3) white corraling of Indian stock; (4) threats of violence; (5) abridgement of rights; and (6) the desire to have the right to elect their own chiefs.[41] For the most part, Olegario's requests were much the same as those voiced by Chief Panto in 1856 when questioned by Burton. Agent Ames was impressed with Olegario's sincerity and filed a report clearly documenting the wishes of the Indians. He also made a strong plea that the Indians be given the aid and considerations they requested. It had become clear to Ames that he was not dealing with an inferior race but rather with a people who had a great deal of pride, people who wished for peace and fairness from the federal government.

When Olegario met with Ames again on July 3, General B.R. Cowan, assistant secretary of the interior, attended the meeting. Ames later reported that Cowan was favorably impressed with Olegario and his captains and was "hopeful of their future if they were to be regarded as specimens of the Mission Indians."[42] Of Olegario, Ames wrote:

> He is intelligent, above the average, peaceably disposed toward the whites, capable of controlling his Indians — for he is virtually chief, notwithstanding the action of the late superintendent — and is at the same time an enthusiastic defender of his people and disposed to take advanced grounds on questions of their rights. A more competent man altogether cannot be found in the tribe.[43]

Following his meetings with Olegario and a series of trips that took him to various Indian villages, Ames forwarded a report to the commissioner of Indian affairs. In this report, Ames detailed the grievances of Olegario and his people and restated the dire need for a reservation. The report reminded the commissioner that the United States had not lived up to the terms of the Treaty of Guadalupe Hidalgo, and further stated that as a result of the government's inaction, Indians were falling into a state of increased degradation. Ames cited widespread prostitution, alcohol abuse, and loss of will.[44] Ames also stressed that little of any earlier appropriations for California Indians had reached San Diego County Indians.

Commissioner of Indian Affairs Edward P. Smith, another missionary appointed by President Grant, considered the Ames report to be one that warranted immediate action. Smith stated in his annual report that the government must act to rectify past wrongs perpetrated against Indians by establishing tracts of land where their rights could be guaranteed and where they could attempt to exist without white harassment.[45] The reports of Smith and Ames were forwarded to Congress for approval of an appropriation of $50,000 and the establishment of a reservation system. Congress established a committee to make recommendations regarding these requests. As happened so often before, the requests were denied by the committee for Indian affairs. In rejecting the requests for land and money, the chairman of the committee, Senator Oglesby, lashed out at the entire Indian affairs system, making it clear that he and his committee had little time or money to spend on what they considered to be "barbarous savages."[46]

Assessing the land situation in California, Oglesby noted that no land was available to Indians unless they first became citizens and went through the homestead and preemption process or moved to one of the already established reserves. Oglesby's statement regarding Indian citizenship is ironic because Indians in southern California could not easily become citizens. Three Indians, including a Pala Indian, Pedro Pablo, who had been steadily employed in Los Angeles for several years, had recently applied for United States citizenship with the Los Angeles county clerk.[47] They were refused citizenship, and although their attorney, Christopher N. Wilson, appealed to the United States commission at Los Angeles seeking further action, that appeal was later denied.[48]

Indian efforts to attain citizenship were met frequently by incredulous blank stares, bureaucratic inaction, and the inability of local administrators to reach a consistent decision. It may have seemed to whites, who had for so long considered Indians as second class persons, that citizenship was out of the question although they were at a loss to state why this was so. In light of the bloody subjugation of the Modoc Indians of northern California in June 1873, resulting from the Modoc Lava Bed Battles and the elimination of the Modoc leaders, it may have justifiably occurred to Olegario and his people that the federal government was far more willing to wage war than to provide land or seek peace. Instead of some concrete, positive move on the part of the government, the rejection of the Ames proposals again left the Indians and their agents in a quandary.

In his annual report of 1874, Commissioner Edward P. Smith noted that Congress had rejected Ames' recently proposed plan and stated that little was being done for the Indians except the appointment of yet another investigator who was to contact all of the Indians of San Diego County, assess their needs and make a report to Congress.[49] Smith also stated that Special Commissioner Charles A. Wetmore, was attempting to find land that might be set aside for the exclusive use of the Indians although nothing absolute had been accomplished. Nine years after the Civil War ended, and twenty-four years after they were first recommended, Congress had not approved a reservation system for San Diego. In spite of the earnest efforts of President Grant, his six commissioners of Indian affairs, and various government agents interested in implementing reform through the Grant Peace Policy, the Native Americans of San Diego County were increasingly becoming homeless aliens in their own land. As the cool breezes of fall 1874, blew across the coastal hills of San Diego, the wheels of government ever so gradually ground on toward setting tracts of land aside for native use. Indeed, it would be another year before the reservations were actually established.

Chapter VIII

Compression and Containment:
Adoption of a Reservation System, 1874-1880

Appointed in 1874, Special United States Commissioner of Mission Indians Charles A. Wetmore laid the foundation of a new era for Indians in San Diego County. In years past the government had made treaties without provision for their implementation, and Indians had been ungenuinely assured that land would be set aside for their exclusive use. Under the Grant administration, Congress and the Department of the Interior made earnest efforts to deal with the issue of native land rights. Yet not until 1874 did such efforts produce results, and these largely emerged with the arrival on October 13, 1874 of Commissioner Wetmore. As soon as he set foot in San Diego, Wetmore began an immediate investigation into the cause of the conflicts between Indians and Anglos. After interviewing several native leaders and white settlers, Wetmore concluded that up until fall of 1867 the Indians had been relatively unmolested and unhampered by whites. Wetmore agreed with B.C. Whiting that "Southern California...remained in the pastoral condition until about the fall of 1867, when a reaction took place in public sentiment, and California was sought for homes."[1]

As a result of the sudden influx of white settlers and drifters, Olegario and other Native Americans in San Diego County felt the thrust of the Anglo quest for land. Addressing himself to earlier, unsuccessful attempts of the government to aid the Indians, including the reservation order of 1870, Special Commissioner Wetmore echoed the anguish voiced by Olegario and his people. He decried previous "ineffectual attempts to reserve public lands for Indians" and complained that the "opposition and protests of white settlers" had successfully defeated several proposals for reservations.[2] As late as September 7, 1873, the **San Diego Union** had carried an editorial opposing the establishment of reservations and noting that a majority of whites opposed such efforts. The **Union** concluded that: "The land is for the people who can cultivate it and become producers, adding to the prosperity of the commonwealth, and the Indians must go."[3] Echoing the tune of Manifest Destiny, the **Union** asserted that a proposed reservation at San Pasqual "would be a failure. It would be resisted by the Indians, and it would be a gross outrage upon the farmers of that section."

In a final self-righteous blast, the editor stated that not only should the Indians be kept off land currently occupied by whites but that Indians should be forbidden from any land "likely to be so occupied by whites within the next twenty years."[4]

Realizing that the success of his policies would rest on their acceptance by the local Anglos, Wetmore held an informal meeting with prominent white men interested in solving what they termed, the "Indian problem." On October 20, 1874, in the San Diego County Court House, Wetmore addressed a large group, including County Judge Thomas H. Bush; lawyer and past owner of the **San Diego Union**, Charles P. Taggart; Assemblyman William W. Bowers; Major D. Chase; District Attorney Albert Beecher Hotchkiss; Judge J.W. Tyson; County Clerk Grant; Sheriff Nicholas Hunsacker; and developer, A.E. Horton.[5] For Wetmore the meeting proved a success and his reception assured him the eventual adoption of his policies. Those participating in the meeting reacted favorably toward his plan. Wetmore's plan called for the survey of all public lands so that the claims and rights of whites and Indians would be firmly established. He planned to set aside certain lands for Indians which would be protected from white intrusion. To further the government's "civilization" policies, Wetmore wanted schools, churches, and other institutions to be established for Indians, to ensure that they had means and ways by which they could "uplift" themselves.[6] Following the meeting, various southern California newspapers, including the **San Diego Union, La Cronica**, and the **National Republican** gave their endorsements.

In the interval between submission of Wetmore's report and government approval of his recommendations, conditions worsened for Indians. The continuing failure of the federal government to establish a reservation system in San Diego County was, by 1875, hastening the cultural, economic, and social decline of the Indians. The continued loss of territory deprived Indians of food resources, water rights, and land rights. In his annual report for 1875, Indian Affairs Commissioner Edward P. Smith maintained that "all available agricultural lands have been seized or occupied by individual [white] owners."[7] Smith's view was supported by other white officials. In a field report written in June 1875, to Commissioner Smith, Special Agent D.A. Dryden stated that in all of the places he had visited, Indian land in southern California was rapidly falling into the hands of whites. According to Dryden, Indian gardens were "being invaded and their pastures consumed by the stock of white settlers; the water turned away from their ditches to irrigate the gardens of those trespassing upon their lands; and they have no redress."[8] Concluding his report, Dryden pleaded with the federal government to set aside tracts of lands for the Indians. His requests went unheeded. As report after report stacked up on polished desks in Washing-

Maria la Cruz, a Diegueno woman of Mesa Grande, March, 1920. Courtesy Museum of the American Indian.

ton, Olegario and other Indian leaders retained their faith in Wetmore and Dryden, sincerely believing that the favorable policies advocated by white agents would eventually be enacted. Still, they worried about the continuing settlement of whites in San Diego.

Following a plan based on Wetmore's recommendations, the government commissioned County Surveyor James Pascoe to survey certain tracts of land situated in the northern part of San Diego County as part of an overall plan to investigate the possibility of purchasing land for Indians. As Pascoe conducted his field work in July 1875, he encountered Olegario's resistance. The Indian leader had seen the consequences of allowing government surveyors to make their maps, believing that once mapped, the government would open the lands to white settlement and use the map as a legal document to assert governmental rights to the land. The Indian leader had also heard rumors that even if Pascoe mapped an Indian reserve, it would encompass only his people's rancherias and the small gardens surrounding them. Olegario's position was best explained by Pascoe in July 1875. Pascoe reported that he "went to Olegario's camp, at the Rincon in Pauma Valley where the chief said that he would allow no survey to be made of any one of the rancherias occupied by his people, without first calling them together, explaining the matter to them and having their consent and permission."[9] Pascoe attempted to persuade Olegario that it was in his people's best interest to allow the survey, but his pleas were unsuccessful. Pascoe noted that Olegario stood his ground without violence, but "there was an evident determination on the part of Olegario to impede the progress of any steps that did not meet with his consent or approval."[10]

The fear that still more land was to be taken from Indians became a harsh reality on September 9, 1875, when Sheriff Nicholas Hunsaker served a writ of eviction against Olegario and the Temecula Indians. According to the writ, three ranchers from San Francisco identified only as Murietta, Saujarjo, and Pujol, had asked the fifteenth circuit court for legal title to certain lands surrounding the Temecula Valley. The court had granted permission for these ranchers to occupy such lands and evict the Indians if they saw fit.[11] On September 10, Hunsaker served Olegario with the writs to ensure that the Indian leader was aware of the proceedings. Olegario was given until September 20 to prepare the tribe for removal. Initially, Hunsaker reported that the Indians accepted the writ of eviction stoically and without protest. However, when Hunsaker returned on the 20th, the Indians refused to leave. They asked for an extension of time so that they could consult with Olegario who was in Los Angeles seeking legal advice. Hunsaker replied that no further consultation was necessary and that the Indians would have to vacate. In an effort to calm the increasingly bitter Indians, Murietta offered a 40-day extension to allow Indians time to harvest their crops and make final preparations for the move. In return, Murietta asked them to sign a contract, agreeing to the extension but assuring that they would vacate on a designated date.[12]

Not having a command of English and fearing that they were signing something which gave up their claims to the land, only a third — about seven families — signed the documents. In an editorial on the matter, the **San Diego Union** made a veiled reference to Olegario and Attorney Wilson, declaring that the refusal of the Indians to sign Murietta's paper was the result of continuing bad advice from persons in Los Angeles. The newspaper asserted that once the Indians clearly understood the hopelessness of further delay, they would abandon the land without any trouble. The **Los Angeles Express** also followed the Temecula controversy, indicating an awareness of Olegario's visit to Los Angeles. The tone of the article was less optimistic than that of the San Diego paper and far more sympathetic to the Indians. Describing the eviction, the paper predicted that the Indians, "will be deprived of their property, and driven from their homes, at the very commencement of the worst season of the year."[13] Aware of Olegario's situation and the despair of his people, the **Express** condemned white actions and the inaction of the federal government: "Every year the Government sends an Agent to palaver with the Indians; he comes, has his palaver, and makes a report to the Secretary of the Interior; the report is deposited in a pigeon hole in the Indian Bureau, and that is the end of it."[14]

Although the **Los Angeles Express** and other observers were aware of the discontent and despair of the Indians, the **San Francisco Alta** remained oblivious to the growing restlessness of Indians in San Diego County. The **Alta** ignored the Indians' increasingly desperate situation and placed the blame for Indian anger and frustration on their legal counsel. Speaking of Christopher N. Wilson, the Indians' Los Angeles lawyer, the **San Francisco Alta** asserted that the attorney for the Indians "has for a long time been trying to induce the Mission Indians to believe that they were American citizens, entitled to vote, preempt land, etc. The Indians have also been led to believe that they could not be ejected from lands, which they occupied without any known title. They were encouraged to believe that they had all the rights of American citizens, as well as the privileges claimed for Indians."[15]

Taking a broader approach, the **San Diego Union** declared that both Indians and whites possessed land rights and that eviction of Indians at Temecula was a simple matter of white men claiming what was "legally" theirs. The editor criticized those who stood in the way of the "legal" eviction. In particular, the editor pointed the finger of blame at the federal government for allowing its agents to fill the Indians' heads with erroneous thoughts regarding their title to land. Also at fault was, according to the **Union**, Attorney Wilson who represented the Indians as if they actually had equal legal status and absolute land rights. As a final solution to the Indian problem, the **Union** suggested that Wetmore's plan be adopted and set into motion.[16]

Amidst this flurry of editorials, Agent Dryden wrote a terse letter to Sheriff Hunsaker, stating that the eviction left him powerless to aid the Indians and lamented that he could "provide only minimal relief for the landless Indians."[17] A dispatch in the **San Francisco Bulletin** noted that Dryden had held a meeting with Olegario and his captains, finding them "much dejected and exasperated."[18] From the San Luis Rey-Pala area, County Supervisor F. Estudillo informed the **San Diego Union** that trouble loomed in northern San Diego County and that Olegario had made violent threats that included armed warfare and the burning of local homes and stores.[19] Estudillo's claims were never substantiated but they fed the fires of frontier rumor. After a week of fearing an impending attack, the **San Diego Union** lashed out at the United States Army who refused to send military aid to put down the non-existent war. Speaking of the refusal, the **Union** made some cryptic allusions to the recent campaigns at Modoc Lava Beds that led to the crushing defeat of the Modoc people, implying that rapid and forceful actions of that type were well-suited in San Diego County.[20]

The **San Diego Union** printed a letter dated October 5, 1875, that stated there were no signs of Indian wars or a threat of violence from Olegario. Yet, the newspaper insisted that war was imminent and that the situation called for strong measures. While the **San Francisco Alta**, blamed the Indians' despair on the government, "Indian lovers," and an incompetent agent, the **San Diego Union** saw the root of the problem in Olegario's defiance.[21] Since the common concept of a good Indian in the nineteenth century was a dead Indian, it is likely that the editors of the newspaper advocated war, particularly when one editor stated that "Olegario, the 'chief', is a bad Indian and if he was suppressed we should have no more Indian trouble."[22] In the case of Olegario's lawyer, C.N. Wilson, there is little doubt what the **San Francisco Alta** had in mind when it stated that "The Indian chief, Olegario, is the client of a Los Angeles lawyer who ought to be treated to a dose of martial law, if such were possible."[23] Indians had few rights and many whites opposed any effort to inform them of legal options. In spite of evidence to the contrary, throughout most of October, various newspapers and local correspondents asserted that Olegario was about to go on the warpath and planned attacks on San Luis Rey and Monserrate. Much of this concern was based on a single conversation with one Indian woman, as well as Anglo anxieties, and alarmist gossip spread

Trinidad Duro was an elder from the Mesa Grande Reservation. She was a respected leader. San Diego Museum of Man.

by Manual Cota's followers.[24] Whether Olegario was actually planning any overt acts is uncertain, although no evidence exists to support the idea except rumors and the general fear of Anglos who knew they were outnumbered.

Regardless of the intent of Olegario, settlers and ranchers in northern San Diego County assumed the worst and herded their livestock, boarded up their houses, moved to population centers, and requested military support. Stirred by sensational newspaper accounts and a sincere fear of another major uprising, much of the north county area was temporarily in the hands of the belligerent Indians who had never fired a shot. In an article in the **San Diego Union**, Agent Dryden reportedly looked upon the Indian situation as a grave matter. He blamed the United States government for not empowering him to aid the Indians in any way and asserted that he was unable to give them encouraging promises for the future.[25] In response, the **Los Angeles Express** lashed out at federal Indian policy, stating that "our Indian system is a fraud — disgraceful to the Government and humiliating to every right thinking citizen."[26] Addressing the problem of squatters and settlers who had fomented the bogus uprising, the editor of the **Express** inquired why no blame was attached to the men who confiscated Indian land thus displacing "a large family of peaceful and industrious Indians who are now legally remanded to a life of vagrancy."[27] The **Express** offered a solution similar to Wetmore's plan. The editor suggested that the United States buy select portions of land which had once been the home of the Indians, and establish a reservation.

While editors penned vitriolic barbs, Olegario increasingly believed that whites intended to take the remaining land of his people in return for empty promises and meaningless pieces of paper. That Olegario had assessed the situation correctly was revealed by a statement made by Agent Dryden. In a letter to the **Los Angeles Express**, in which he defended his actions and motives during the recent turmoil in north San Diego County, the Reverend Dryden explained that "There is no legal recognition of their [the Indians] title to lands anywhere, and no protection by the Government... when land was plenty and cheap, but there was but little trouble, but there is not one of their settlements but what is either included in the survey of some ranch or being covered by settlers."[28] Dryden concluded his letter, prophesizing that "it will be but a short time when scarcely an acre of tillable land will be left to them [the Indians] in all of Southern California." The Indians, Dryden asserted, would "either be driven to desperation, retaliation and speedy extermination, or left to wander as harmless mendicants."[29] The prophesy partially explains the torment and anguish of those Indian leaders, such as Olegario, who attempted to stem the advancing tide of Anglo settlers.

The **Sacramento Record Union** raised the wrath of the **San Diego Union** when editors of the Sacramento paper favored formalized recognition of Indian land rights. In October 1875, the San Diego newspaper called the Sacramento tabloid, "uninformed." The **San Diego Union** quoted the northern paper as stating that troops had justifiably not been provided for the so-called Olegario Uprising and that a lack of troops might force the whites to deal with the Indians more fairly. The **Record Union** further asserted that the Luisenos at Temecula "have heretofore been quiet and well-conducted, and there is no ground for supposing that they would have taken the warpath had they been justly treated."[30] The **Record Union**, like the **Los Angeles Express** placed the major portion of the blame on the federal government's inaction and neglect, adding that the desire of whites in San Diego to answer the Indians with guns was unreasonable and ill-conceived.

Offended by the Los Angeles and Sacramento papers, the **San Diego Union** issued an editorial that absolved itself and local whites from the charge of calling for bloodshed and causing animosity on the part of the Indians. The editor placed blame on the federal government and the fact that they had "given title to a Rancho [sic] partly occupied by these poor people, and has failed to provide for the Indians who have been made homeless by its own act."[31] As far as overstating the case, as the **Sacramento Record Union** charged, the San Diego editor again rebuked the upstate newspaper and insisted that "conflict may occur at any moment between the desperate Indians immediately under the control of Olegario and some of the people in the vicinity."[32]

While Anglo anxieties and editorial rhetoric increased, Olegario slipped off to Los Angeles for more legal consultation. Two weeks later, the **San Diego Union** confessed that things had not been quite as bad as it had earlier thought. Refusing to admit that the Indians had never planned an insurrection, the **Union** explained that "Olegario was merely blustering, and could not bring his Indians up to the fighting pitch, and that the danger was not so great as represented by Supervisor Estudillo."[33] Yet, the **Union** maintained that although the situation was overstated, white fears of Indian violence were real.

Perhaps because of the earlier scare in 1871 and Olegario's continued resistance, the **Union** finally, and without explanation, endorsed a plan for a reservation system in San Diego County. In an article on October 19, 1875 the **Union** noted that Olegario was in Los Angeles again "circulating a petition of some sort" and that there was little more one could say about the Indian problem except that the government should adopt a plan "making immediate provision for the Indians. Congress should make the needful appropriation to carry into effect such a plan without delay."[34] There was irony in the **Union**'s statement. For over twenty years, as Indians steadily lost acre after acre of prime land to Anglo squatters and settlers, the **Union** maintained a strong anti-reservation stance through editorials laced with the white man's Manifest Destiny. Finally, when the Indians had lost nearly all claims to their lands, been burned out of San Pasqual, evicted from Temecula and constantly threatened with violence, the **Union** admitted that something must be done about the "Indian problem" and that the government should act without delay.

Assured by Agent Dryden and Special Inspector E.C. Kemble that the government would take rapid and sure steps to gain land for the Indians, Olegario stayed in the Los Angeles area, laboring at the vineyard of Don Mateo Keller, a prominent Los Angeles businessman and old friend of the chief. The **Los Angeles Star** noted that Kemble had left for Arizona on his way to Washington, D.C., and that he would be making "a strong appeal to the government in behalf of the tribe of which Olegario is chief."[35] To ensure that the government acted with minimal delay, Olegario also traveled to Washington. The **San Diego Union** of November 9, 1875, reported that Olegario was on his way to the nation's capital for an interview with President Grant.[36] One week later Olegario had his talk with Grant and the **San Diego Union** stated that the President had "promised temporary relief to the ejected Indians, and said that he would recommend Congress to provide a permanent home for them."[37]

President Grant, still in pursuit of his Indian Peace Policy and acting on the advice of local and federal agents, proved true to his word in contrast to past government officials. On December 27, 1875 he issued an executive order that set aside lands in San Diego County for the exclusive use of Native Americans. Included in this executive order were the reservations of Santa Ysabel, Pala (refer to Plate 1), Agua Caliente, Sequan, Inaja, Cosmit, Potrero, Cahuilla, and Capitan Grande.[38] In total, the Indians secured 52,400 acres, or slightly more than three quarters of the 69,000 acres granted in 1870 and revoked in 1872 (Figure 3). The government set aside another 6000 acres for southern California Indians in May 1876. Through this later executive order, Grant added 640 acres to Potrero and 880 acres to Agua Caliente. After years of adversity, Grant's Peace Policy and Indian land reform finally arrived in San Diego County immediately after the dismissal of Commissioner of Indian Affairs Edward P. Smith and during the first two weeks of the tenure of Commissioner John Q. Smith.[39] John Smith was the last commissioner appointed by Grant, and he witnessed the dying throes of the sometimes successful, frequently stymied Peace Policy.

Over the next two years Olegario served his people well. He constantly protested the encroachments of Anglo settlers on land that his tribe claimed or was seeking for reservation land. He made numerous trips to San Diego and Los Angeles, trying in vain to convince various local, state, and federal officials that his people were entitled to a recognized plot of land and protection from the whites. When Olegario realized that he had little legal recourse he tried to assert his claims with force, as in the case of Portrero which Margarita Trujillo had owned through an old Spanish land grant known as Cuca Rancho. She had allowed Indians to live on the property and had little or no trouble with them. In June 1877, she subleased a large portion of the tract to Antonio Varela of Los Angeles. Varela intended to graze thousands of head of cattle on the lush grasses that grew in the Potrero region. Olegario heard of the transaction and realized that thousands of head of cattle would mean a continued depletion in the food resources of his people, plus an influx of animals and men that might crowd his people even closer together and off of the fertile land from which they made their living.

When Varela arrived at Cuca, Olegario gathered a force of about 50 followers and put Varela off the ranch. In response, Varela had a number of the Indians arrested and arraigned before Justice Cave Couts, who

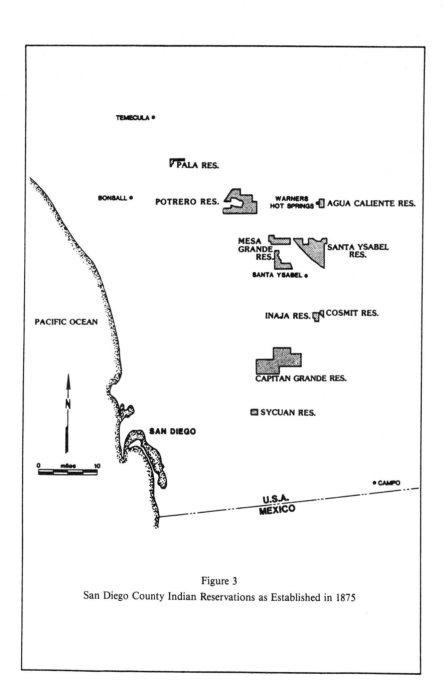

Figure 3
San Diego County Indian Reservations as Established in 1875

released the Indians claiming that he had no jurisdiction. Flushed with victory and believing that they had finally won a major battle, the Indians returned to the rancho to inform Margarita Trujillo that she must also leave. In a newspaper account of the incident, the **San Diego Union** pleaded for a proper agent with the authority to control matters, which in their mind meant eviction of the Indians in the same manner that they had been removed from Temecula.[40] Olegario's stand for his people's traditional land at Cuca was too strident for local leaders and ranchers. Almost in unison they, and the **San Diego Union**, sought Olegario's arrest, demanding that Indians living on the Cuca Rancho be immediately evicted.[41] On July 14, 1877, Deputy Sheriff Ed Bushyhead, himself part Cherokee, served papers on Olegario. While at Pala, Bushyhead was threatened by Olegario's men.[42] After several tense hours of confrontation between Bushyhead and Olegario, the deputy was allowed safe passage out of Pala. Bushyhead served the papers, but the Indians ignored them.

Within a week Olegario was in San Diego presenting his case to Judge Moses A. Luce.[43] Olegario protested that the Cuca band had lived on the land since time began and that the Mexican government had recognized Luisenos as rightful owners of their rancheria within the rancho. Judge Luce promised that he would investigate the matter but said he doubted if any land beyond reservation boundaries would be considered as Indian-owned. Tension between whites and Luisenos gradually increased in July 1877. Amid white appeals to the federal government and growing resentment of Olegario, the Luisenos' leader died mysteriously in his sleep on July 31, 1877. Hurt and angry, Olegario's followers claimed that he had been poisoned by either scheming whites or resentful members of Manuel Cota's band.[44] Indians requested an autopsy, and Coroner T.C. Stockton and Justice Couts performed the examination, reportedly finding no evidence of foul play. To this day local Luisenos dispute the findings of the coroner and judge.[45]

With the death of Olegario, a significant chapter in Native American history closed. Jose Chanate, a well-intended but ineffectual leader, was elected to replace Olegario.[46] Without the dynamism and forcefulness of a strong leader like Olegario, Luisenos at Pala and Rincon gradually withdrew inward to the reservations developing an isolationist policy. Leadership returned to the local clan or village level, and the wider sphere of influence — once controlled by Olegario — faded as individual reservations sought to survive in Victorian America. Seven months after Olegario's death, a group of non-reservation Luisenos from the village at San Luis Rey (Plate 2) sought relief from the federal government. Unable to afford the trip to Washington and unsure of themselves in the white political world, disenchanted leaders drafted a letter to the secretary of the interior on February

Luiseno Village at San Luis Rey, circa 1865. Courtesy Los Angeles Public Library.

7, 1878.[47] The Indians complained that they had lost their lands, were being physically abused by whites and feared that they were being left to die in spite of the various treaties and words offered by the agents and government officials.

In rather poignant terms, the Indians requested that they be given even a little land so that they might raise their crops and cattle unmolested. Endowed with a rich cultural heritage and an overwhelming sense of pride, Luisenos sought to convince the government that they were not seeking charity. The Indians implored:

> We do not ask...for the Government to give us money, nor blankets, nor seeds; only some lands for us to cultivate for the support of our families, and to raise our animals to work our lands, and that this land shall be protected against whites and that you hold a protection over us so that it cannot be taken from us.[48]

The letter brought no relief to the San Luis Rey Indians. With the establishment of reservations earlier at Pala and San Pasqual, the government considered the quest for land as a resolved issue. As they had done for decades across the United States, Indian agents made no provisions for tribal territory or ancestral lands and expected the San Luis Rey people to move to another triblet's territory at Pala or San Pasqual.

After thirty years of federal government efforts, Indians of San Diego County had finally gained only minimal recognition of their land rights and, as it was waning, some sparse benefits from Grant's ill-fated Peace Policy. In response to their pleas for a guarantee of land rights, Indians in San Diego County had been removed from many of their tribal villages and given less than 60,000 acres of often unsuitable reservation land that was frequently occupied by Anglo squatters and subject to legal disputes. Situated on land that was only as productive as the water that flowed across it, the Indians were forced to live on land often barren and dry as a result of upstream whites who diverted the available water. Treated as a homogeneous group, which they were not, Indians would be expected to move on-to reservations that were little more than tenuously-recognized plots of land.

Although expected to pay taxes and subscribe to the laws of the land, Indians were not allowed the rights of United States citizens or given the chance to become citizens. Grant's last commissioner, John Q. Smith, advocated citizenship for Native Americans, but he was certainly in the minority and was unsuccessful in implementing his policy.[49] Lacking rights, Indians were treated as wards of the government and forced to rely on a dole, often administered unevenly, slowly, and badly. Once placed on reservations, the Indians would be expected to be largely self-supporting at a time when their culture had been seriously weakened and many of their leaders demoralized by government efforts to destroy Indian self-determination.

Had the government established the reservations in the late 1860s or early 1870s, as had been suggested, Indians might have possessed more and better land, would not have gone through an additional ten years of cultural deprivation, and may have retained more leaders who could have offered a sense of unity and pride to the people. Instead, large segments of the Indian population were seriously demoralized when they finally secured "legal" rights to the land that their people had lived on for over a thousand years. As seems to have often been the case with federal government Indian relations during the latter half of the nineteenth century, the government waited too long to offer too little after asking too much.

Chapter IX

And Still They Endure

As the first months of 1880 unfolded, the Indians of San Diego captured a glimpse of what the next decade held in store for them. The perspective was not bright or encouraging. On January 17, 1880, President Rutherford B. Hayes issued an executive order, cancelling the almost one thousand-acre reservation at Agua Caliente (Warner Hot Springs) that had been set aside in 1887 and removing nearly two thousand acres of the Santa Ysabel Reservation established in 1875.[1] These lands were returned to the public domain at the request of several Anglo settlers who later gained title to the open land. Further south, near the international border at Jacumba, a pitched battle between occupants of a Tipai village and local ranchers left 15 native men and women dead.[2] Now known as the McCain Massacre, the brief skirmish led to Native American abandonment of the Jacumba area and migration into Mexico.

A new era had dawned for the Indian peoples. Once prominent in local economics and noticeable in local affairs, natives gradually gave up many, but certainly not all, of the traditional settlements. Some moved to reservations. Others settled in white communities, attempting to acculturate into a new world. With the establishment of reservations, most federal officials considered the so-called Indian problem solved. Government efforts began to concentrate on providing meager supplies to their reservation-bound wards and implement "its vision of cultural imperialism and execute its work of destructive beneficence."[3] With the taming of the "Wild West" and placement of Indians on reservations, missionaries and do-gooders — such as Helen Hunt Jackson — descended upon the natives. Depicted as noble savages trapped on reservations with little chance of survival in late nineteenth century America, southern California Indians were frequently written off as doomed, in spite of their physical and cultural resilience.[4] Anthropologists from Berkeley to New York visited the reservations, documenting what many of them considered to be the final spasmodic movements of a dying culture, The Vanishing Race! The early work of these anthropologists was known as salvage ethnology, as the carcass of a Native American culture was about to be discarded and the few remaining, func-

Jim Qualsch, Ipai-Tipai, with funeral images, circa 1918. Courtesy Museum of the American Indian.

tioning parts were diligently recorded and studied. Although the period of salvage ethnology, native containment on reservations, and increased native dependence on government wardship is beyond the scope of this analysis, the foundations and antecedents should be easily perceived in the foregoing chapters. The events encompassed in the period from 1850 to 1880 marked the destructive passage of a Native American culture through interaction with the dominant, intrusive Anglo culture.

Throughout the years 1850 to 1880, whites subjected the Indians of San Diego County to American laws, codes, attitudes, and actions designed to make Indians second-class persons. Whites blocked Indians from advancing economically, denying them property rights, water rights, employment, and equal rights under the law. Although certain inactions on the part of Anglos can be attributed to benign neglect and the inabilities of nineteenth century American government to govern, the increased denigration of the Indian in this period was usually the result of conscious anti-Indian actions and legislation. Anglo-American racism, cultural misunderstanding, fear of foreigners (in this case natives), and philosophies based on Manifest Destiny worked covertly and overtly against Native Americans.[5] By virtue of type of employment, marginal social status, government inaction and mismanagement at all levels, anti-Indian sentiment, and racism, the Indians of San Diego County were not allowed citizenship or the chance to establish themselves within the economy or social order of the dominant white race. The typical Anglo response to the growing plight of the Indians was to make vague — usually insincere — attempts to placate them, pacifying them briefly with an occasional "gift" before pushing them out of the way of the rapidly encroaching dominant society. A report, prepared by a special agent investigating the condition and status of Indians in San Diego County, provides a succinct analysis of the point. According to Agent John G. Ames, "this once prosperous and contented people, who had made very successful progress in civilization, are now indigent and homeless wanderers; who have been dispossessed of their lands by white settlers, and made outcasts, dependent upon charity and the meager wages that their labor yields."[6]

Some American Indians successfully acculturated into the dominant white society, seeking to find work, stability, and a better life for their children. Because of federal, state, and local laws, the chance of a given Indian, let alone large numbers of them, breaking out of this increasingly gray world was extremely limited. The failure of the various governmental agencies to deal fairly with Indians did not develop because of the lack of cooperation on the part of Indian leaders. Men such as Olegario and Panto of the Luisenos and Juan Antonio of the Cahuilla attempted to secure land and a lasting agreement with the government. The failure of the treaties of 1852, revocation of the 1870 Pala and San Pasqual reservations, frequently

Five men from Mesa Grande during Eagle Ceremony, 1907. Courtesy San Diego
Historical Society.

shifting boundaries on the later reservation system, and the efforts of the
federal government to suppress self-determination, left Native Americans
disillusioned with, and cynical about, the government.

The Indians of San Diego continued to resist the Anglo world. With the
exception of hardened prostitutes, alcoholics, and others caught up in the
avarice that often developed on the American frontier, most Indians sought
meaning and fulfillment in their own way of life at a time when appeasement
and cultural disintegration were far easier. Generally peaceful throughout
this period, most Indian leaders strove to understand the American legal
process and work within it.

The culture of the Indians adjusted, adapted, and, most significantly,
persisted. By the 1880s, many Americans believed, if not hoped, that Indians would soon vanish from the face of the earth. Once removed from
their native homelands and confined to small tracts of lands known as reservations, many whites felt that Indians and non-western cultures would simp-

ly disappear. Conservatives preferred that the Indians die off, but reformers wished to transform Indians into whites by "civilizing" and Christianizing the peoples they considered savage heathens. However, this was not to be. Indians grasped tenaciously to many of their beliefs, clinging ferociously to their "Indianness."[7] And so it was for the Indians of San Diego. Despite all the adversities, discrimination, and racism, the Indians have persisted as a people and comprise an integral element of San Diego County to this day, even if they are strangers in a stolen land.

FOOTNOTES

CHAPTER I

[1]Notable exceptions to this are George Harwood Phillips, **Chiefs and Challengers** (Berkeley: University of California Press, 1975); Lowell John Bean and Katherine Siva Saubel, **Temalpakh** (Morongo Indian Reservation: Malki Indian Press, 1972); Delfina Cuero, **Autobiography of Delfina Cuero: A Diegueno Indian,** as told to Florence Shipek and translated by Rosalie Robertson (Morongo Indian Reservation: Malki Museum Press, 1970); Harry C. James, **The Cahuilla Indians** (Los Angeles: Westernlore Press, 1960).

CHAPTER II

[1]For works dealing more specifically with the San Dieguito see Julian Hayden, "Restoration of the San Dieguito Type Site to Its Proper Place in the San Dieguito Sequence," **American Antiquity** 31 (January 1966):439-40; James R. Moriarty, "The San Dieguito Complex: Suggested Environmental and Cultural Relationships," **Anthropological Journal of Canada** 7 (Fall 1969): 2-18; Claude N. Warren and D.L. True, "The San Dieguito Complex and Its Place in California Prehistory," **University of California Los Angeles Archaeological Survey Annual Reports 1960-1961,** pp. 246-91; Malcolm Rogers, **Ancient Hunters of the Far West,** ed. Richard Pourade (San Diego: Union-Tribune Publishing Company, 1966). More general works include Claude N. Warren **et al.,** "Early Gathering Complexes of Western San Diego County," **University of California Archaeological Survey Annual Report 1960-1961,** pp. 1-108.

[2]The La Jolla culture pattern is a localized complex associated with the widespread Early Milling Horizon. Archaeological sources for the Early Milling Horizon in general include William J. Wallace, "A Suggested Chronology for Southern California Coastal Archaeology," **Southwestern Journal of Anthropology** 11 (1955):214-30) and Claude N. Warren, "Cultural Tradition and Ecological Adaptation on the Southern California Coast,"

Eastern New Mexico University Contributions in Anthropology 1 (December 1968):1-14. Professional studies on the La Jolla culture began in 1929, Malcolm Rogers, "The Stone Art of the San Dieguito Plateau," American Anthropologist 31 (July-September 1929):454-67, and have continued including Warren, "Early Gathering;" Mabel Harding, "La Jollan Culture," El Museo 1 (July 1951):10-38; James R. Moriarty, et al., "Scripps Estate Site I (SDi-525): A Preliminary Report on an Early Site on the San Diego Coast," University of California Archaeological Survey Annual Reports 1958-1959, pp. 185-216.

[3]In publications spanning several decades, D.L. True has provided several serious studies of the question of early occupation of San Diego's inland valleys. See True, "An Early Complex in San Diego County, California," American Antiquity 23 (January 1958):225-263.

[4]Delbert L. True, "Archaeological Differentiation of Shoshonean and Yuman Speaking Groups in Southern California" (Ph.D. dissertation, University of California, Los Angeles, 1966).

[5]Ibid.

[6]See D.L. True "Investigation of a Late Prehistoric Complex in Cuyamaca Rancho State Park, San Diego County, California," Department of Anthropology Publications, University of California, Los Angeles, 1970.

[7]Alfred L. Kroeber, Handbook of the Indians of California, Bureau of American Ethnology, Bulletin 78 (Washington, D.C.: Government Printing Office, 1925); Robert F. Heizer and M.A. Whipple, The California Indians (Berkeley: University of California Press, 1957). In older anthropological and historical literature, the Yuman-speaking people of San Diego have been called the Northern and Southern Dieguено by Kroeber, Handbook, Plate 57; Heizer and Whipple, The California Indians, map 1. Throughout the 1970s and early 1980s, it became common, although perhaps incorrect, to refer to these people as the Kumeyaay for both Northern and Southern Dieguено as cited by Ken Hedges, "Notes on the Kumeyaay," The Journal of California Anthropology 2 (Summer 1975):71; Florence Shipek, "Kumeyaay Socio-Political Structure," The Journal of California and Great Basin Anthropology 4 (Winter 1982):296-297. Margaret Langdon's, "Kamia and Kumeyaay," The Journal of California Anthropology 2 (Summer 1975):69 reported that the term Kumeyaay was in common use locally as a political term and as a sign of local tribal unity to differentiate them from the Ipai and Tipai. More recently, several researchers have classified the Northern Dieguено as Ipai and the Southern Dieguено/Kumeyaay as Tipai, Katharine Luomala, "Tipai-Ipai," Handbook of North American Indians,

8:592-608 or labeled the Southern Diegueno as Kumeyaay/Tipai to separate them from the Northern Diegueno/Ipai. See Richard L. Carrico, "The Struggle for Native American Self-Determination in San Diego County," **Journal of California and Great Basin Anthropology** 2 (Winter 1980) Figure 1. See also Kroeber, **Handbook**, Plate 57; Heizer and Whipple, **The California Indians**, map 1; Ken Hedges, "Notes on the Kumeyaay,":71.

[8]Kroeber, **Handbook**, pp. 694-95; for thorough studies of Cahuilla food sources and ethnobotany see David Prescott Barrows, **The Ethnobotany of the Coahuilla Indians of Southern California** (Chicago: University of Chicago Press, 1900) and Lowell J. Bean and Katherine Siva Saubel, **Temalpakh** (Banning, California: Malki Museum Press, 1972), and Henry T. Lewis, **Patterns of Indian Burning in California: Ecology and Ethnohistory** (Ramona: Ballena Press, 1973). Ethnographic studies of the Late Milling cultures include Constance DuBois, "Ceremonies and Traditions of the Diegueno Indians," **Journal of American Folk-Lore** 21 (1908):228-236; Edward W. Gifford, "Clans and Moieties in Southern California," **University of California Publications in American Archaeology and Ethnology** 14 (March 1918):155-219; Philip S. Sparkman, "The Culture of the Luiseno Indians," **University of California Publications in American Archaeology and Ethnology** 8 (August 1908):187-234. A recent compilation of ethnographic sources will provide the researcher with sources, repositories, and rarely used documents, see Lowell J. Bean and Sylvia Brakke Vane, **California Indians: Primary Resources; A Guide to Manuscripts, Artifacts, Documents, Serials, Music and Illustrations**, Ramona: Ballena Press, 1977.

CHAPTER III

[1]A well reasoned overview of the early spread of European diseases is provided in Alfred W.Crosby, Jr., **The Columbian Exchange** (Westport, Connecticut: Greenwood Publishing Company, 1972). A more recent work has dealt more specifically with the introduction of diseases to the Sonoran Desert and New Spain, see Henry F. Dobyns, **From Fire to Flood**, Ballena Press Anthropological Papers, 20 (Socorro: Ballena Press, 1981), pp. 45-56.

[2]Sherburne F. Cook, **The Conflict Between the California Indian and White Civilization**, vol. 21: **Ibero-Americana** (Berkeley: University of California Press, 1943).

[3]Letter of Luis Jayme, O.F.M., San Diego, October 17, 1772," in **Baja Travel Series**, ed. Maynard Geiger (Los Angeles: Dawson's Book Shop, 1970), pp. 43-44.

[4]Cook, **Conflict**, vol. 23, pp. 13-55.

[5]Crosby, **The Columbian Exchange.**

[6]Lewis, **Patterns of Burning,** pp. xxxi-xxxii.

[7]Geiger, "Letter of Luis Jayme," p. 39.

[8]Cook, **Conflict,** vol. 23, pp. 6-18; Imre Sutton, "Land Tenure and Changing Occupance on Indian Reservations" (Ph.D. dissertation, University of California at Los Angeles, 1964), pp. 44-45.

[9]U.S. Congress, House Executive Document 41, **Notes on a Military Reconnaissance from Fort Leavenworth in Missouri to San Diego, in California,** by William H. Emory. 30th Congress, 1st session, 1848 (Washington: Wendell and Van Benthuysen, 1848). Reprinted with introduction and notes, Ross Calvin, ed., **Lieutenant Emory Reports** (Albuquerque: University of New Mexico Press, 1951), p. 165.

[10]Ibid., p. 181.

[12]Henry F. Dobyns, ed., **Hepah, California: The Journal of Cave Johnson Couts from Monterey, Neuvo Leon, Mexico to Los Angeles, California during the Years 1848-1849** (Tucson: Arizona Pioneers' Historical Society, 1961), pp. 85-86.

[13]Ibid., p. 90.

[14]U.S. Department of the Interior, Office of Indian Affairs, **Report of Charles A. Wetmore, Special United States Commissioner of Mission Indians of Southern California,** 1875, p. 4.

[15]Ibid.

[16]Cook, **Conflict,** vol. 23, pp. 1-94.

[17]Robert F. Heizer and Alan F. Almquist, **The Other Californians** (Berkeley: University of California Press, 1971), p. 22.

[18]Jack D.Forbes, **Native Americans of California and Nevada** (Heraldsburg: Naturegraph Publishers, 1969), p. 61.

[19]George Harwood Phillips, **Chiefs and Challengers** (Berkeley: University of California, 1975), pp. 20-70.

CHAPTER IV

[1]See Hubert Howe Bancroft, **Bancroft's Works,** vol. 7: **History of California** (San Francisco: The History Company, 1886) pp. 474-80; Jack D. Forbes, ed., **The Indian in America's Past** (Englewood Cliffs: Prentice-Hall,

1964); Theodora Kroeber, **Ishi in Two Worlds** (Berkeley: University of California Press, 1961), pp. 56-101.

²Bancroft, **History of California,** p. 477.

³Horace Bell, **Reminiscences of a Ranger** (Los Angeles: Caystile and Mathes, 1881), p. 116.

⁴**San Diego Herald,** August 6, 1853.

⁵**San Diego Herald,** April 17, 1852; William E. Smythe, **The History of San Diego** (San Diego: The History Company, 1908), p. 185; **San Diego Herald,** February 17, 1855.

⁶Los Angeles Star, August 30, 1851.

⁷Ibid.

⁸U.S. Department of the Interior, Office of Indian Affairs, **Reports on Indian Affairs 1861-1871,** "Report of A.P. Greene," February 20, 1871, p. 342.

⁹Cook, **Conflict** pp. 84-85.

¹⁰**Reports on Indian Affairs, 1861-1871,** p. 342.

¹¹Cook, **Conflict,** pp. 86-87.

¹²**San Diego Herald,** April 17, 1852.

¹³U.S. Department of the Interior, Office of Indian Affairs, **Annual Report of the Commissioner of Indian Affairs for the Year 1870,** p. 91.

¹⁴**San Diego Herald,** February 17, 1855.

¹⁵**Statutes of California,** 1850 (San Jose: J. Winchester, 1850), p. 409.

¹⁶**San Diego Herald,** October 7, 1853.

¹⁷Ibid., December 13, 1856.

¹⁸Ibid.

¹⁹Rufus K. Porter and C.S. Crosby, "History of Spring Valley," written in 1886-1887 for Hubert H. Bancroft, San Diego Historical Society Library and Manuscripts Collection, San Diego, California, pp. 7-8.

²⁰Coroner's Inquest Reports, 1870-1880, File No. 277, January 29, 1873, San Diego Historical Society Library and Manuscripts Collection; **San Diego Union,** February 1, 1873.

²¹Ibid.

²²County Clerk Certificates of Death, Box 1, San Diego Historical Society Library and Manuscripts Collection, San Diego, California.

²³Coroner's Inquest Reports, 1870-1880, File No. 287, June 14, 1875.

²⁴**San Diego Union,** June 13, 1875 and June 15, 1875.

²⁵Coroner's Inquest Reports, File No. 287.

²⁶Johnson, Saum and Knobel Mortuary Book," September 17, 1875, San Diego Historical Society Library and Manuscripts Collection.

²⁷Ibid., November 5, 1880.

²⁸Coroner's Inquest Reports, 1870-1880, File No. 23, June 27, 1878.

²⁹**San Diego Union,** June-September 1877.

³⁰Coroner's Inquest Report 1870-1880, File No. 59-1/2, August 5, 1877.

³¹Ibid., November 2, 1877; The Daily Journal of Frank Frary, April 19, 1877, San Diego Historical Society Library and Manuscripts Collection, San Diego, California.

³²Helen Hunt Jackson, **A Century of Dishonor** (Boston: Roberts Brothers, 1887), p. 471.

³³**San Diego Union,** December 12, 1879.

³⁴Tamar Elizabeth Bevington, "As I Remember," typescript, California Room, San Diego Public Library, 1925, pp. 6-7.

³⁵Ibid., p. 6.

³⁶**San Diego Herald,** April 17, 1852.

³⁷San Diego City Ordinance File, Ordinance 5, Section 1, San Diego Historical Society Library and Manuscripts Collection, San Diego, California.

³⁸City Police Docket 1874-1883: San Diego, California, San Diego Historical Society Library and Manuscripts Collection, San Diego, California.

³⁹Ibid. For an analysis of Indians and legal repression in Los Angeles during this era, see George Phillips, "Indians in Los Angeles, 1781-1875: Economic Integration, Social Disintegration," **Pacific Historical Review** 46 (August 1980):441-451.

⁴⁰Document File, Indigents. San Diego Historical Society Library and Manuscripts Collection, San Diego, California.

[41]Ibid.

[42]**San Diego Union,** January 11, 1874.

[43]**San Diego Union,** 1874-1880; personal communication with Dr. Paul H. Ezell, Director, Presidio de San Diego excavations.

[44]Johnson, Saum and Knobel Mortuary Book." San Diego Historical Society Library and Manuscripts Collection, San Diego, California, January 10, 1870 to November 3, 1880.

[45]Ibid.

[46]San Diego County Reports," Box File, San Diego Historical Society Library and Manuscripts Collection, San Diego, California.

[47]Albert L. Hurtado, "Hardly a Farm House—A Kitchen Without Them: Indian and White Households on the California Borderland Frontier in 1860," **The Western Historical Quarterly** (July 1982) pp. 245-70.

[48]**San Diego Herald,** October 8, 1853.

[49]**San Diego Herald,** November 11, 1854.

[50]**San Diego Union,** January 7, 1875; January 10, 1875.

[51]**San Diego Herald,** February 9, 1856.

[52]Benjamin D. Wilson, **The Indians of Southern California in 1852,** ed., John W. Caughey (San Marino: Huntington Library Press, 1952), p. 149.

[53]Ibid., p. 21.

[54]Bevington, "As I Remember," p. 8.

[55]Ibid., p. 3.

[56]U.S. Department of the Interior, Office of Indian Affairs, **Report of Charles A. Wetmore, Special United States Commissioner of Mission Indians of Southern California, 1875,** p. 5.

[57]Augustus S. Ensworth Ledger, San Diego Historical Society Library and Manuscripts Collection, San Diego, California, p. 106.

[58]Frank Kimball Diary: 1877, March 11, 1877, National City Public Library Archives, National City, California.

[59]George McKinstry Diary: 1860, San Diego Historical Library and Manuscripts Collection, San Diego, California.

[60]Ibid.

[61] Joseph Foster Diary: 1874-1880, Serra Museum and Library, San Diego, California.

[62] Ibid.

[63] Anonymous Diary of E.W. Morse Mining Operations in Baja California, San Diego Historical Society Library and Manuscripts Collection, San Diego, California.

[64] Ibid.

[65] U.S. Census Bureau, **8th Census, 1860, Population Schedules: San Diego, California**. See Hurtado, "Hardly a Farm House," pp. 245-70.

[66] City Police Docket 1874-1882, San Diego Historical Society Library and Manuscripts Collection, San Diego, California.

[67] A.J. Chase to E.W. Morse, San Francisco, June 2, 1866, San Diego Historical Society Library and Manuscripts Collection, San Diego, California.

[68] Ibid., July 5, 1866.

[69] Joseph Smith Letter File, Document of Indenture executed by William H. Noyes, Justice of the Peace, December 16, 1861, San Diego Historical Society Library and Manuscripts Collection, San Diego, California.

[70] **8th Census, 1860, Population Schedules: San Diego, California.**

[71] Wilson, **Indians in 1852,** p. 103 and 149; Jackson, **Century of Dishonor,** p. 458.

[72] Benjamin Hayes, "California Miscellany: Pioneer Notes," Bancroft Library, Berkeley, California, p. 430.

[73] Wetmore, **Special Report,** p. 4.

CHAPTER V

[1] Josiah Royce, **California, A Study of American Character** (New York: Alfred Knopf, 1948), pp. 217-18.

[2] Charles S. Cushing, "The Acquisition of California, Its Influence and Development Under American Rule," **California Law Review** 8 (January 1920):71.

[3] Helen Hunt Jackson, "Report on the Condition and Needs of the Mission Indians of California," reprinted as Appendix XV, **A Century of Dishonor** (Boston: Roberts Brothers, 1887), pp. 458-514; Wilcomb E. Wash-

burn, **The Indian and the White Man** (Garden City, New York: Anchor Books, 1964), pp. 307-407; Wendell Oswalt, **This Land Was Theirs** (New York: John Wiley and Sons, 1973), pp. 560-581. Excellent discussions of California Indian legal status are provided by Chauncey S. Goodrich, "Legal Status of the California Indian," **California Law Review** 14 (January 1926):83-100, and by Ferdinand F. Fernandez, "Except A California Indian: A Study in Legal Discrimination," **Southern California Quarterly** 50 (Fall 1968):161-75.

[4]Fernandez, "Except a California Indian," p. 164.

[5]**Statutes of California: 1850** (San Jose: J. Winchester, 1850), p. 408.

[6]Ibid.

[7]Ibid., p. 409.

[8]Ibid., p. 410.

[9]Bancroft, **History of California 6,** p. 164.

[10]**Statutes,** p. 409.

[11]Heizer and Almquist, **The Other Californians**p. 40; Cook, **Conflict pp. 4-20.**

[12]**Statutes,** p. 409.

[13]**Statutes of California: 1851** (Vallejo: G. Kenyon Fitch, 1851), Chapter 49, Section 1.

[14]Jackson, "Report on the Conditions," pp. 458-514.

[15]**Statutes,** p. 409.

[16]Fernandez, "Except a California Indian," p. 166.

[17]**Statutes,** p. 408.

[18]County Court, Santa Cruz County, California. People vs. Juan Antonio. **Supreme Court of California Docket 27 California 404**.

[19]**Statutes of California: 1854** (Sacramento: B.B. Redding, 1854), p. 24.

[20]**Statutes of California: 1855** (Sacramento: B.B. Redding, 1855), pp. 229-37.

[21]Fernandez, "Except a California Indian," p. 167.

[22]Ibid.

[23]Goodrich, "Legal Status," p. 94.

CHAPTER VI

[1]U.S. Congress, Senate, Luke Lea to Adam Johnson, Washington, D.C., April 14, 1849, Senate Document 4, 33rd Congress, Special Session, 1849, p. 2.

[2]Ibid.

[3]Harry Kelsey, "The California Indian Treaty Myth," **Southern California Quarterly** 55 (Fall 1973):229-300.

[4]Ibid., p. 230.

[5]Ibid., pp. 230-31.

[6]**San Diego Herald,** September 9, 1851.

[7]John Walton Caughey, **California,** 2nd edition (New York: Prentice-Hall, 1940), p. 382; Phillips, **Chiefs and Challengers,** contains a thorough discussion of the Garra uprising.

[8]**San Diego Herald,** January 10, 1852; Dr. O.M. Wozencraft, "Statement," 1877, Indian Affairs 1849-1850, C-D 204, Bancroft Library, Berkeley, pp. 10-13.

[9]**San Diego Herald,** January 10, 1852; Charles Kappler, ed., **Indian Affairs: Laws and Treaties, 1778-1883** (New York: Interland Publishing Company, 1972), 5:1127-28.

[10]U.S. Congress, Senate, Oliver M. Wozencraft to Luke Lea, Middle District, California, February 18, 1852, Senate Executive Document 4, 33rd Congress, Special Session, 1852, pp. 287-88.

[11]Robert F. Heizer, **The Eighteen Unratified Treaties of 1851-1852** (Berkeley: Archaeological Research Facility, 1972), pp. 56-57; Alban W. Hoopes, **Indian Affairs and Their Administration, 1849-1860** (Philadelphia: University of Pennsylvania Press, 1932), pp. 44-45.

[12]Kelsey, "Treaty Myth," p. 231; Heizer, **Unratified Treaties,** pp. 4-5.

[13]Heizer, **Unratified Treaties,** p. 5.

[14]Kelsey, "Treaty Myth," pp. 4-5.

[15]**Congressional Globe,** March 26, 1852, p. 890.

[16]California Legislature, Governor John Bigler, "Special Message to the Senate and Assembly of the State of California," January 30, 1852. **Journal of the Third Session of the Legislature of California** (G.K. Fitch and Company, and V.E. Geiger and Company, State Printers, 1852), p. 80.

[17]California Legislature, "President of the Senate Samuel Purding seeking rejection of the Indian Treaties," February 11, 1852. **Journal of the Third Session of the Legislature of California** (G.K. Fitch and Company, and V.E. Geiger and Company, State Printers, 1852), p. 106.

[18]**Los Angeles Star,** 13 March 1852.

[19]Benjamin D. Wilson, **The Indians of Southern California in 1852,** ed., John W. Caughey (San Marino: Huntington Library Press, 1952), p. xxv.

[20]Wozencraft to Lea, Senate Executive Document 4, p. 289.

[21]**Los Angeles Star,** December 18, 1852.

[22]Heizer, **Unratified Treaties,** p. 5; Wilson, **Indians of California,** p. 16.

[23]Hoopes, **Indian Affairs,** pp. 45-46.

[24]**San Diego Herald,** June 23, 1855.

[25]Ibid., March 18, 1854.

[26]Ibid., May 23, 1854.

[27]Ibid., July 14, 1855.

[28]U.S. Congress, House, H.S. Burton to Major E.D. Townsend, Mission San Diego, January 27, 1856, **Report on the Mission Indians,** House Executive Document 76, 34th Congress, 3rd Session, 1856, p. 115.

[29]California. **Journals of Senate and Assembly of the Sixteenth Session of the Legislature,** Report of W.E. Lovett, Special Indian Agent to Austin Wiley (O.M. Clayes, State Printer, 1866) 3:4.

[30]Lyle C. Annable, "The Life and Times of Cave Johnson Couts, San Diego County Pioneer" (Master's thesis, San Diego State University, 1965), pp. 73-74.

[31]Hoopes, **Indian Affairs,** p. 56.

[32]**San Diego Herald,** 23 June 1855.

[33]Cave J. Couts to Colonel Thomas J. Henley, July 7, 1856. Reprinted in **San Diego Herald,** August 2, 1856.

[34]Ibid.

[35]Benjamin Ignatius Hayes, **Pioneer Notes,** ed., Marjorie T. Wolcott (Los Angeles: Private Printing, 1929), p. 161. Major Blake's efforts were reported in the **Los Angeles Star,** June 13, 1857.

[36]**San Diego Herald,** August 2, 1856.

[37]Michael A. Sievers, "Malfeasance or Indirection? Administration of the California Indian Superintendency's Business Affairs," **Southern Cali fornia Quarterly** 56 (Fall 1974):280.

[38]Ibid, pp. 277-80. An overview of the federal policies in general is provided in Robert A. Trennert, Jr., **Alternative to Extinction: Federal Indian Policy and the Beginnings of the Reservation System, 1846-51** (Philadelphia: Temple University Press, 1975).

[39]Burton to Townsend, p. 114.

[40]Ibid.

[41]Ibid., p. 115.

[42]U.S. Congress, House, H.S. Burton to Captain D.R. Jones, Mission San Diego, June 15, 1856, House Executive Document 76, 34th Congress, 3rd Session, 1856, p. 127.

[43]U.S. Department of the Interior, Office of Indian Affairs, **Annual Report of the Commissioner of Indian Affairs for the Year 1859,** p. 6.

[44]John Ross Browne, **The Tribes of California** (San Francisco: Colt Press, 1947), p. 8.

[45]U.S. Department of the Interior, Office of Indian Affairs, **Annual Report of the Commissioner of Indian Affairs for the Year 1865,** pp. 141-44.

[46]**Annual Report 1865,** Lovett to Wiley, May 1865, p. 122.

[47]For an example of such fears of disloyalty, see William Coffin to Abraham Lincoln, **Robert Todd Lincoln Collection of the Papers of Abraham Lincoln,** comp. Robert T. Lincoln (Washington, D.C.: Government Printing Office, 1959), p. 1.

[48]Lt. Thomas E. Turner to Major W.S. Ketchum, San Bernardino, October 5, 1861. Typescript on file San Diego Historical Society Library and Manuscripts Collection, San Diego, California.

[49]**Wilmington Journal,** May 13, 1865.

[50]Cave J. Couts to Ephraim Morse, Guajome, May 28, 1864, Ephraim Morse Letter file, San Diego Historical Society Library and Manuscripts Collection, San Diego, California.

[51]**Annual Report 1865,** Lovett to Wiley, May 1865, p. 123.

[52]**Wilmington Journal,** May 13, 1865.

[53]U.S. Department of the Interior, Office of Indian Affairs, **Annual Report of the Commissioner of Indian Affairs for the Year 1865,** J.Q.A. Stanley to Austin Wiley, March 28, 1865, p. 287.

[54]**Annual Report 1865,** Austin Wiley to William P. Dole, April 12, 1865, pp. 286-287.

[55]U.S. Department of the Interior, Office of Indian Affairs, **Annual Report of the Commissioner of Indian Affairs for the Year 1865,** J.Q.A. Stanley to Austin Wiley, May 19, 1865, p. 295.

[56]California Legislature, **Appendix to Journals of Senate and Assembly.** 16th Session, 1866, "Report of W.E. Lovett, Special Indian Agent, to Austin Wiley, Superintendent of Indian Affairs in California," p. 5.

[57]Ibid., pp. 6-7.

[58]B.C. Whiting quoted in Marjorie McMorrow Rustvold, "San Pasqual Valley: From Rancheria to Greenbelt" (Master's thesis, San Diego State University, 1968), p. 96. Special Agent J.J. Kendrick had reported a similar problem with alcohol and Anglo traders in 1857, as reported in the **Los Angeles Star,** September 26, 1857.

[59]**San Diego Herald,** June 26, 1869, quoting the **San Francisco Alta.**

[60]Ibid.

[61]William Henry Ellison has provided a concise overall account of the federal Indian policy in California during the 1846-1860 period in his "The Federal Indian Policy in California, 1846-1860," **Mississippi Historical Review** 9 (June 1922):37-67.

CHAPTER VII

[1]Cave J. Couts to Edward F. Beale, San Francisco, May 8, 1852, Letters Received by the Office of Indian Affairs, 1824-1881, California Superintendency, 1849-1880, 1849-1852. Microcopy 234, Roll 32, United States National Archives.

[2]**San Diego Herald,** August 2, 1856; also cited in Benjamin D. Wilson, **The Indians of Southern California in 1852,** ed. John W. Caughey (San Marino: Huntington Library Press, 1952), p. xxv.

[3]**Los Angeles Star,** November 29, 1856; Earlier in the same year the **Star** suggested that the Cahuilla at San Gorgonio deserved a reservation and recommended that 1280 acres of good agricultural land be set aside for them, **Los Angeles Star,** June 21, 1856.

⁴**Los Angeles Star,** "Indians of the South," clipping noted as Fall 1858, Benjamin Hayes Scraps, Bancroft Library, Berkeley, California.

⁵U.S. Department of the Interior, Office of Indian Affairs, **Reports on Indian Affairs, California Superintendency, 1861-1871,** "Annual Report of Special Agent J.Q.A. Stanley," Los Angeles, California, August 5, 1866, p. 102.

⁶U.S. Department of the Interior, Office of Indian Affairs, **Reports on Indian Affairs 1861-1871,** "Report of Special Agent J.Q.A. Stanley," Southern California, March 1867, p. 114.

⁷Ibid., p. 115.

⁸Ibid.

⁹U.S. Department of the Interior, Office of Indian Affairs, **Annual Report of the Commissioner of Indian Affairs for the Year 1867,** p. 9; An excellent discussion of the roles and policies of various Commissioners of Indian Affairs for the post Civil War period including Reverend Taylor, is provided in Kvasnicka and Viola, ed., **The Commissioners,** pp. 109-50.

¹⁰U.S. Department of the Interior, Office of Indian Affairs, **Annual Report of the Commissioner of Indian Affairs for the Year 1868,** B.C. Whiting to N.G. Taylor, San Francisco, California, October 10, 1868, p. 588.

¹¹Ibid.

¹²Kvasnicka and Viola, **The Commissioners,** pp. 116-20.

¹³A comprehensive analysis of Grant's Peace Policy and later Indian reform movements is presented in Francis Paul Prucha, **American Indian Policy In Crisis: Christian Reformers and the Indian, 1865-1900** (Norman: University of Oklahoma Press, 1976), pp. 30-60.

¹⁴U.S. Department of the Interior, Office of Indian Affairs, **Annual Report of the Commissioner of Indian Affairs for the Year 1869,** p. 459.

¹⁵Ibid., p. 629.

¹⁶U.S. Congress, House, **Letter from the Secretary of the Interior Regarding Indian Reservations in San Diego County,** House Executive Document 296, 41st Congress, 2nd Session, 1870, pp. 1-2.

¹⁷Benjamin Hayes, "Scrapbooks," Volume 32, "Indians," Volume 1, Report of Special Agent Augustus P. Greene, San Pasqual Valley Reservation, April 10, 1870, Bancroft Library, Berkeley, California, p. 78.

¹⁸**Reports on Indian Affairs, 1861-1871,** "Annual Report of Brigadier

General J.B. McIntosh, United States Army," San Francisco, California, July 13, 1870, p. 73.

[19]**San Diego Union,** March 10, 1870.

[20]Ibid., April 21, 1870.

[21]**San Francisco Alta,** April 9, 1870.

[22]**Reports on Indian Affairs, 1861-1871,** "Annual Report of Lieutenant A.P. Greene, United States Army," San Pasqual Valley Reservation, August 30, 1870, p. 92.

[23]U.S. Department of the Interior, Office of Indian Affairs, **Annual Report of the Commissioner of Indian Affairs for the Year 1865,** J.Q.A. Stanley to Austin Wiley, March 28, 1865, p. 295.

[24]Cave J. Couts to Manuel Cota, Rancho Guajome, September 1, 1853, Cave J. Couts Collection, "Indian Affairs," CT297, Huntington Library, San Marino.

[25]For a brief history of Olegario's life in Los Angeles and the aid he received from two influential men, see Richard L. Carrico, "Wolf Kalisher: Immigrant, Pioneer Merchant and Indian Advocate," **Western States Jewish Historical Quarterly,** 15 (January 1983):99-106.

[26]Hayes, "Scrapbooks," Volume 38, "Indians," Volume 1, Manuelito and Olegario Controversy, San Diego, California, October 4, 1871, p. 244.

[27]**San Diego Union,** July 7, 1870.

[28]Hayes, "Scrapbooks," Volume 38, "Indians," Volume 1, pp. 243-44.

[29]Ibid., p. 243.

[30]Ibid., p. 244.

[31]U.S. Department of the Interior, Office of Indian Affairs, **Reports on Indian Affairs, 1861-1871,** "Annual Report of Brigadier General J.B. McIntosh," p. 73.

[32]U.S. Department of the Interior, Office of Indian Affairs, **Annual Report of the Commissioner of Indian Affairs to the Secretary of the Interior for the Year 1886,** E.S. Parker to C. Delano, February 13, 1871.

[33]U.S. President, **Proclamations and Executive Orders, 1862-1938** (Washington, D.C.: Government Printing Office, 1975).

[34]U.S. Department of the Interior, Office of Indian Affairs, **Reports on**

Indian Affairs, "Annual Report of A.P. Greene, Special Agent Mission Indian Agency," February 20, 1871, p. 342.

[35]**San Diego Union,** August 24, 1871; August 31, 1871; September 7, 1871; **Los Angeles Star,** August 30, 1871.

[36]**San Diego Union,** October 26, 1871.

[37]Ibid., September 28, 1871.

[38]Ibid., November 2, 1871.

[39]Hayes, "Scrapbooks," Volume 28, "Indians," Volume 1, Petition to B.C. Whiting, Superintendent of Indian Affairs, undated.

[40]**San Diego Union,** March 29, 1872.

[41]U.S. Congress, House, **Mission Indians of Southern California,** "Report of John G. Ames," House Executive Document 91, 43rd Congress, 1st Session 1874, pp. 4-5.

[42]Ibid., p. 7.

[43]Ibid.

[44]Ibid., pp. 4-16.

[45]Ibid., p. 2; Commissioner Smith was a staunch supporter of the reservation system and sought the containment of wandering, landless Indian bands. Smith fought a largely unsuccessful battle for Grant's Peace Policy at a time when it was under heavy attack (see especially Kvasnicka and Viola, **The Commissioners,** pp. 143-45).

[46]U.S. Congress, Senate, Committee on Indian Affairs, **Report on the Mission Indians of California.** Senate Report 180, 43rd Congress, 1st Session, 1874, pp. 1-2.

[47]**Los Angeles Star,** June 1873.

[48]"Report of John G. Ames," p. 11.

[49]U.S. Department of the Interior, Office of Indian Affairs, **Annual Report of the Commissioner of Indian Affairs for the Year 1874,** p. 382.

CHAPTER VIII

[1]U.S. Department of the Interior, Office of Indian Affairs, **Report of Charles A. Wetmore, Special U.S. Commissioner of Mission Indians of Southern California,** 1875, p. 5.

[2]Ibid.

[3]**San Diego Union,** September 7, 1873.

[4]Ibid.

[5]**Report of Charles Wetmore,** p. 11.

[6]Ibid., p. 8.

[7]U.S. Department of the Interior, Office of Indian Affairs, **Annual Report of the Commisisoner of Indian Affairs to the Secretary of the Interior for the Year 1875,** p. 10.

[8]Ibid., p. 223.

[9]**San Francisco Alta,** October 13, 1875, "Olegario's Revolt."

[10]Ibid.

[11]**San Diego Union,** September 24, 1875.

[12]Ibid.

[13]**San Diego Union,** September 23, 1875, quoting the **Los Angeles Express.**

[14]Ibid., also see **Los Angeles Evening Express,** September 17, 1875.

[15]**San Diego Union,** October 8, 1875, quoting the **San Francisco Alta.**

[16]**San Diego Union,** October 3, 1875.

[17]Ibid.

[18]**San Francisco Bulletin,** September 29, 1875.

[19]**San Diego Union,** October 3, 1875.

[20]**San Diego Union,** October 5, 1875.

[21]**San Diego Union,** October 7, 1875.

[22]Ibid.

[23]**San Diego Union,** October 8, 1875.

[24]**San Diego Union,** October 12, 1875.

[25]Ibid.

[26]**Los Angeles Evening Express,** October 7, 1875.

[27]Ibid.

[28]**Los Angeles Evening Express,** October 8, 1875.

[29]Ibid.

[30]**San Diego Union,** October 13, 1875, quoting the **Sacramento Record Union.**

[31]**San Diego Union,** October 13, 1875.

[32]Ibid.

[33]Ibid.

[34]**San Diego Union,** October 19, 1875.

[35]**Los Angeles Star,** October 24, 1875.

[36]**San Diego Union,** November 9, 1875.

[37]Ibid., November 20, 1875.

[38]Ibid., January 23, 1875.

[39]Kvasnicka and Viola, **The Commissioners,** pp. 149-53.

[40]**San Diego Union,** June 27, 1877.

[41]Ibid.

[42]Ibid., July 14, 1877.

[43]Ibid., July 17, 1877.

[44]**San Diego Union,** August 4, 1877.

[45]Interview with Native American informants, Pala and Pauma Reservations, San Diego County, California, June 1976-December 1977.

[46]**San Diego Union,** August 18, 1877.

[47]Ibid., February 10, 1878.

[48]Ibid., August 18, 1877.

[49]Kvasnicka and Viola, **The Commissioners,** pp. 149-153.

CHAPTER IX

[1]U.S. Department of the Interior, Office of Indian Affairs, **Annual Report of the Commissioner of Indian Affairs to the Secretary of the Interior, 1886,** p. 307.

²Peter R. Odens, **The Desert's Edge** (Yuma: Sun Graphics, 1977), pp. 97-100.

³Kvasnicka and Viola, ed., **The Commissioners,** p. 170.

⁴Works typical of this "noble savage" period include Helen H. Jackson's, "The Present Condition of the Mission Indians in Southern California," **Century Magazine,** August 1883, pp. 511-29, her **Century of Dishonor** (Boston: Roberts Brothers, 1887), and her **Report of Mrs. Helen Jackson and Abbott Kinney on the Mission Indians in 1883** (Boston: Stanley & Usher Press, 1887), and Charles Painter's, **A Visit to the Mission Indians of Southern California** (Philadelphia: Indian Rights Association, 1886).

⁵J.E. Chamberlain, **The Harrowing of Eden: White Attitudes Toward Native Americans** (New York: Seabury Press, 1975).

⁶U.S. Congress, House, **Mission Indians of Southern California,** "Report of John G. Ames," House Executive Document 91, 43rd Congress, 1st Session, 1874, p. 1.

⁷Edward H. Spicer, "Persistent Cultural Systems," **Science** 174 (November 1971), pp. 795-800. Lowell J. Bean, Henry F. Dobyns, M. Kay Martin, Richard W. Stoffle, Sylvia Brakke Vane, and David R.M. White, "Persistence and Power, A Study of Native American Peoples in the Sonoran Desert and the Devers to Palo Verde High Voltage Transmission Line" (Rosemead: Southern California Edison Co., 1978).

BIBLIOGRAPHY

A. Primary Sources

Manuscript Collections

San Diego, California. San Diego Historical Society Library and Manuscripts Collection.

San Diego, California. County Clerk Certificates of Death, 1850-1880.

San Diego, California. San Diego Historical Society Library and Manuscripts Collection. Indigents Document File.

San Diego, California. San Diego Historical Society Library and Manuscripts Collection. Johnson, Saum and Knobel Mortuary Book. 1869-1888.

San Diego, California. San Diego Historical Society Library and Manuscripts Collection. San Diego City Ordinance File.

San Diego, California. San Diego Historical Society Library and Manuscripts Collection. City Police Docket. 1874-1883.

San Diego, California. San Diego Historical Society Library and Manuscripts Collection. San Diego County Reports.

Diaries, Letters, and Narratives

Berkeley, California. Hubert H. Bancroft Library. Benjamin Hayes Papers. "California Miscellany: Pioneer Notes."

Berkeley, California. Hubert H. Bancroft Library. Benjamin Hayes Scrapbooks. "Indians of the South," Fall 1858.

Berkeley, California. Hubert H. Bancroft Library. "Benjamin Hayes Scrapbooks." Volumes 1, 28, 32.

Berkeley, California. Hubert H. Bancroft Library. Indian Affairs, 1849-1850. C-D 204, Dr. O.M. Wozencraft.

Dobyns, Henry F., ed. **Hepah, California: The Journal of Cave Johnson Couts from Monterey, Nuevo León, Mexico to Los Angeles, California during the years 1848-1849.** Tucson: Arizona Pioneer Historical Society, 1961.

Jayme, Luis. "Letter of Luis Jayme, O.F.M.," in **Baja Travel Series.** Edited by Maynard Geiger. Los Angeles: Dawson's Book Shop, 1970.

Laguna Niguel, California. National Archives. Letters Received by the Office of Indian Affairs, 1824-1881. Microcopy 234, Roll 32. "Cave J. Couts to Edward F. Beals," 8 May 1852.

Lincoln, Robert T. **Robert Todd Lincoln Collection of the Papers of Abraham Lincoln.** Washington: Government Printing Office, 1959.

National City, California. National City Public Library Archives. Frank Kimball Diary. 1855-1913. The Frank A. Kimball Diaries.

San Diego, California. San Diego Historical Society Library and Manuscripts Collection. Augustus S. Ensworth Document File.

San Diego, California. San Diego Historical Society Library and Manuscripts Collection. Ephraim W. Morse Papers.

San Diego, California. San Diego Historical Society Library and Manuscripts Collection. Frank Frary Diaries and Letters. 1875, 1877, 1885, 1887.

San Diego, California. San Diego Historical Society Library and Manuscripts Collection. George McKinstry Diaries, 1859-1879.

San Diego, California. San Diego Historical Society Library and Manuscripts Collection. Joseph Smith Document File.

San Diego, California. San Diego Historical Society Library and Manuscripts Collection. Rufus K. Porter and C.S. Crosby Papers: Spring Valley. Document files.

San Diego, California. San Diego Public Library California Room. Tamar Elizabeth Bevington Papers, "As I Remember San Diego," 1925.

San Marino, California. Huntington Library. Cave J. Couts Collection: Indian Affairs, CT297.

Newspapers

Congressional Globe, 26 March 1852.

Los Angeles Evening Express, 17 September 1875.

Los Angeles Star, 1851-1876.

San Diego Herald, 1852-1864.

San Diego Union, 1870-1880

San Francisco Alta, 13 October 1875.

San Francisco Bulletin, 1875.

Wilmington Journal, 1865.

Government Documents

California. **Appendix to Journals of Senate and Assembly of the Sixteenth Session of the Legislature** (1866).

California. **Journal of the Third Session of the Legislature of California** (1852).

California. **Journal of Senate and Assembly of the Sixteenth Session of the Legislature** (1866).

California. **Statutes** (1850). San Jose: J. Winchester.

California. **Statutes** (1851). Vallejo: G. Kenyon Fitch.

California. **Statutes** (1854). Sacramento: B.B. Redding.

California. **Statutes** (1855). Sacramento: B.B. Redding.

U.S. Census Bureau. **8th Census Population Schedules: San Diego, California,** 1860.

U.S. Congress. House. **Letter from the Secretary of the Interior Regarding Indian Reservations in San Diego County.** House Executive Document 296, 41st Congress, 2nd Session, 1870.

U.S. Congress. House. **Notes of a Military Reconnaissance from Fort Leavenworth in Missouri to San Diego, in California.** House Executive Document 41, 30th Congress, 1st Session, 1848; reprint ed., **Lieutenant Emory Reports.** Albuquerque: University of New Mexico Press, 1951.

U.S. Congress. House. **Report on the Mission Indians.** House Executive Document 76, 34th Congress, 3rd Session, 1856.

U.S. Congress. Senate. Committee on Indian Affairs. **Report on the Mission Indians of California.** Senate Report 180, 43rd Congress, 1st Session, 1874.

U.S. Congress. Senate. Luke Lea to Adam Johnson. Senate Document 4, 33rd Congress, Special Session, 1849.

U.S. Congress. Senate. Oliver M. Wozencraft to Luke Lea. Senate Exeutive Document 4, 33rd Congress, Special Session, 1852.

U.S. Department of the Interior. Office of Indian Affairs. **Annual Reports of the Commission of Indian Affairs for the Years 1865-1886.**

U.S. Department of the Interior. Office of Indian Affairs. **Report of Charles A. Wetmore, Special United States Commissioner of Mission Indians of Southern California,** 1875.

U.S. Department of the Interior. Office of Indian Affairs. **Reports on Indian Affairs, 1861-1871.**

U.S. President. **Proclamations and Executive Orders, 1862-1938.** Washington, D.C.: Government Printing Office, 1975.

Oral Interviews and Native American Consultation

Lucas, Thomas. Kumeyaay Individual. Laguna Ranch and San Diego, California, 1976-1977.

Rodriguez, Henry. Luiseno Tribal Representative. San Diego, California, 1978-1980.

Southcutt, Fern. Native American Advisor. San Diego, California, 1980-1981.

B. Secondary Sources

Books

Bancroft, Hubert H. **The Works of Hubert Howe Bancroft.** Vols. 4-7: **The History of California.** San Francisco: The History Company, 1884-1886.

Barrows, David Prescott. **The Ethnobotany of the Coahuilla Indians of Southern California.** Chicago: University of Chicago Press, 1900.

Bean, Lowell John and Katherine Siva Saubel. **Temalpakh.** Banning, California: Malki Museum Press, 1972.

Bean, Lowell J. and Sylvia Brakke Vane. **California Indians: Primary Resources; A Guide to Manuscripts, Artifacts, Documents, Serials, Music and Illustrations.** Ramona: Ballena Press, 1977.

Bell, Horace. **Reminiscences of a Ranger.** Los Angeles: Caystile and Mathes, 1881.

Browne, John Ross. **The Indians of California.** San Francisco: Colt Press, 1947.

Caughey, John Walton. **California.** 2nd Edition. New York: Prentice-Hall, 1940.

Chamberlain, J.E. **The Harrowing of Eden: White Attitudes Toward Native Americans.** New York: Seabury Press, 1975.

Cook, Sherburne F. **The Conflict Between the California Indian and White Civilization. Ibero-American,** Vols. 21-24. Berkeley: University of California Press, 1943.

Crosby, Alfred W., Jr. **The Columbian Exchange.** Westport, Connecticut: Greenwood Publishing Company, 1972.

Cuero, Delfina. **The Autobiography of Delfina Cuero: A Diegueno Indian.** Translated by Rosalie Robertson and edited by Florence Shipek. Morongo Indian Reservation: Malki Museum Press, 1970.

Curtis, Edward S. **The North American Indian.** Norwood, Massachusetts: Plimpton Press, 1926.

Danziger, Edmund Jefferson, Jr. **Indians and Bureaucrats: Administering the Reservation Policy During the Civil War.** Chicago: University of Illinois Press, 1974.

Dobyns, Henry F. **From Fire to Flood.** Ballena Press Anthropological Papers, 20. Socorro: Ballena Press, 1981.

Forbes, Jack D., ed. **The Indian in America's Past.** Englewood Cliffs: Prentice-Hall, 1964.

_____. **Native Americans of California and Nevada.** Healdsburg: Naturegraph Publishers, 1969.

Hayes, Benjamin Ignatius. **Pioneer Notes.** Edited by Marjorie T. Wolcott. Los Angeles: Private Printing, 1929.

Heizer, Robert F. **The Eighteen Unratified Treaties of 1851-1852.** Berkeley: Archaeological Research Facility. 1972.

Heizer, Robert F., and Alan F. Almquist. **The Other Californians.** Berkeley: University of California Press, 1971.

Heizer, Robert F. and M.A. Whipple. **The California Indians.** Berkeley: University of California Press, 1957.

Hoopes, Alban W. **Indian Affairs and their Administration, 1849-1860.** Philadelphia: University of Pennsylvania Press, 1932.

Jackson, Helen Hunt. **A Century of Dishonor.** Boston: Roberts Brothers, 1887.

_____. **Report of Mrs. Helen H. Jackson and Abbott Kinney on the Mission Indians in 1883.** Boston: Stanley & Usher Press, 1887.

James, Harry C. **The Cahuilla Indians.** Los Angeles: Westernlore Press, 1960.

Kappler, Charles J., ed. **Indian Affairs: Laws and Treaties, 1778-1883.** New York: Interland Publishing Company, 1972.

Kroeber, Alfred L. **Handbook of the Indians of California.** Bureau of American Ethnology Bulletin 78. Washington, D.C.: Government Printing Office, 1925.

Kroeber, Theodora. **Ishi in Two Worlds.** Berkeley: University of California Press, 1961.

Kvasnicka, Robert M. and Herman J. Viola, ed. **The Commissioners of Indian Affairs, 1824-1977.** Lincoln: University of Nebraska Press, 1979.

Lewis, Henry T. **Patterns of Indian Burning in California: Ecology and Ethnohistory.** Ramona: Ballena Press, 1973.

Odens, Peter R. **The Desert's Edge.** Yuma: Sun Graphics, 1977.

Oswalt, Wendell. **This Land Was Theirs: A Study of the North American Indian.** New York: John Wiley and Sons, 1973.

Painter, Charles. **A Visit to the Mission Indians of Southern California and Other Western Tribes.** Philadelphia: Indian Rights Association, 1886.

Phillips, George H. **Chiefs and Challengers.** Berkeley: University of California Press, 1975.

Prucha, Francis Paul. **American Indian Policy in Crisis: Christian Reformers and the Indian, 1865-1900.** Norman: University of Oklahoma Press, 1976.

Rogers, Malcolm. **Ancient Hunters of the Far West.** Edited by Richard Pourade. San Diego: Union-Tribune Publishing Company, 1966.

Royce, Josiah. **California, A Study of American Character.** New York: Alfred Knopf, 1948.

Smythe, William E. **History of San Diego.** San Diego: The History Company, 1908.

Trennert, Robert A., Jr. **Alternative to Extinction: Federal Indian Policy and the Beginning of the Reservation System, 1846-51.** Philadelphia: Temple University Press, 1975.

Washburn, Wilcomb E. **The Indian and the White Man.** Garden City: Anchor Books, 1964.

Wilson, Benjamin D. **The Indians of Southern California in 1852.** Edited by John W. Caughey. San Marino: Huntington Library Press, 1952.

Periodicals and Magazines

Carrico, Richard L. "The Struggle for Native American Self-Determination in San Diego County," **Journal of California and Great Basin Anthropology** 2 (Winter 1980).

_____. "Wolf Kalisher: Immigrant, Pioneer Merchant and Indian Advocate," **Western States Jewish Historical Quarterly** 15 (January 1983).

Cushing, Charles S. "The Acquisition of California, Its Influence and Development Under American Rule." **California Law Review** 8 (January 1920):67-85.

DuBois, Constance. "Ceremonies and Traditions of the Diegueno Indians." **Journal of American Folklore** 21 (1908):228-236.

Ellison, William H. "The Federal Indian Policy in California, 1846-1860." **Mississippi Valley Historical Review** 9 (June 1922):37-67.

Fernandez, Ferdinand F. "Except a California Indian: A Study in Legal Discrimination." **Southern California Quarterly** 50 (Fall 1968): 161-75.

Gifford, Edward W. "Clans and Moieties in Southern California." **University of California Publications in American Archaeology and Ethnology** 14 (March 1918):155-219.

Goodrich, Chauncey S. "The Legal Status of the California Indian." **California Law Review** 14 (January 1926):83-100.

Harding, Mabel. "La Jollan Culture." **El Museo** 1 (July 1951):10-38.

Hayden, Julian D. "Restoration of the San Dieguito Type Site to Its Proper Place in the San Dieguito Sequence." **American Antiquity** 31 (January 1966):439-440.

Hedges, Kenneth. "Notes on the Kumeyaay." **The Journal of California Anthrolopogy** 2 (Summer 1975):71-83.

Hurtado, Albert L. "Hardly a Farm House—A Kitchen Without Them: Indian and White Households on the California Borderland Frontier in 1860." **The Western Historical Quarterly** (July 1982) pp. 245-270.

Jackson, Helen H. "The Present Condition of the Mission Indians in Southern California." **The Century Magazine** 26 (August 1883): 511-29.

Kelsey, Harry. "The California Indian Treaty Myth." **Southern California Quarterly** 55 (Fall 1973):225-38.

Langdon, Margaret. "Kamia and Kumeyaay." **The Journal of California Anthropology** 2 (Summer 1975):69.

Moriarty, James R. "The San Dieguito Complex: Suggested Environmental and Cultural Relationships." **Anthropological Journal of Canada** 7 (Fall 1969):2-18.

Moriarty, James R., George Shumway, and C.N. Warren. "Scripps Estates Site I (SDi-525): A Preliminary Report on an Early Site on the San Diego Coast." **University of California Archaeological Survey Annual Reports 1951**, pp.185-216.

Phillips, George. "Indians in Los Angeles, 1781-1875: Economic Integration, Social Disintegration." **Pacific Historical Review** 46 (August 1980).

Rogers, Malcolm. "The Stone Art of the San Dieguito Plateau." **American Anthropologist** 31 (July-September 1929):454-67.

Sievers, Michael A. "Malfeasance or Indirection? Administration of the California Indian Superintendency's Business Affairs." **Southern California Quarterly** 56 (Fall 1974):273-94.

Sparkman, Philip S. "The Culture of the Luiseno Indians." **University of California Publications in American Archaeology and Ethnology** 8 (August 1908):187-234.

Spicer, Edward H. "Persistent Cultural Systems." **Science** 174 (November 1971):795-800.

Wallace, William J. "A Suggested Chronology for Southern California Coastal Archaeology." **Southwestern Journal of Anthropology** 11 (1955):214-230.

Warren, Claude N. "Cultural Tradition and Ecological Adaptation on the Southern California Coast." **Eastern New Mexico University Contribution in Anthropology** 1 (December 1968):1-14.

Warren, Claude N. and D.L. True. "The San Dieguito Complex and Its Place in California Prehistory." **University of California Los Angeles Archaeological Survey Annual Reports 1960-1961**, pp. 246-338.

Warren, Claude N., D.L. True, and Ardith Eudey. "Early Gathering Complexes of Western San Diego, California: Results and Interpretation of an Archaeological Survey." **University of California Archaeological Survey Annual Reports, 1960-61**, pp. 1-108.

Unpublished Manuscripts

Annable, Lyle C. "The Life and Times of Cave Johnson Couts, San Diego County Pioneer." M.A. Thesis, San Diego State College, 1965.

Bean, Lowell J., Henry F. Dobyns, M. Kay Martin, Richard W. Stoffle, Sylvia Brakke Vane, and David R.M. White. "Persistence and Power, A Study of Native American Peoples in the Sonoran Desert and the Devers to Palo Verde High Voltage Transmission Line." Rosemead: Southern California Edison Company, 1978.

Rustvold, Marjorie. "San Pasqual Valley: From Rancheria to Greenbelt." M.A. Thesis, San Diego State College, 1968.

Sutton, Imre. "Land Tenure and Changing Occupance on Indian
Reservations." Ph.D. Dissertation, University of California at
Los Angeles, 1964.

True, Delbert L. "Archaeological Differentiation of Shoshonean and
Yuman Speaking Groups in Southern California." Ph.D. Dissertation, University of California at Los Angeles, 1966.

INDEX

-A-

Alta California 13
Agua Caliente . . 5,7,35,61,67,84,89
Agua Caliente Reservation 84
Agua Grande 57
Aguanga 35,67
Altithermal Period 6
American Legal System 42
Ames, John G. 72-73, 91
An Act for the Government
  and Protection of Indians
  (California Statute 133) . . 22-23,
    38-39, 41-42, 44
Anathermal Period 6
Antonio, Jose 71
Anza-Borrego Desert 15
Apis, Pablo 53

-B-

Baja California 31
Ballena Valley 31
Bandini, J.B. 71
Banner, George V. 25
Barbour, George W. 45, 47
Beale, Edward F. 50, 51, 60
Bell, Horace 18
Bevington, Tamar E.M. 30
Bigler, John 47
Black Codes 39
Blake, George 52

Bowers, William W. 76
Browne, J. Ross 54
Bureau of Indian Affairs 47,
    51-52, 56, 59, 63, 66, 79
Burton, H.S. 51, 53, 54
Bush, Thomas H. 67, 76
Bushyhead, Edward 86

-C-

Cahuilla . . . 1, 4, 9, 34, 46, 56, 57,
    67, 91
Cahuilla (rancheria) 84
Cahuilla Reservation 84
Cajon 35
California legislature 47
Californios 30
Capitan Grande 35, 84
Carrillo, Ramon 56
Cassiday, Andrew 71
Capitan Reservation 84
Census of 1860 . . . . . 32-33, 35, 37
Chase, D. 76
Chinese 25, 28
Chola 57
Chronological Model for San
  Diego Prehistory and History . 6
Civil War 18, 56, 59, 60, 74
Claudio 27
Common School Act (Indians
  Excluded) 44
Cook, Sherburne F. 21

Cosmit Reservation 84
Cosmopolitan Hotel 29
Cota, Manuel (Ito) . 29, 52-54, 56,
                          66-71, 81, 86
Couts, Cave J. Sr. 15-16, 29,
        50-53, 56, 60, 63, 67, 84, 86
Cowan, B.R. 72
Cox, J.D. 65
Coyotes 57
Crosby, C.S. 23
Cruz, Juan de 25
Cultural History 5-10
Cultural Settings 6
Cushing, Charles S. 37
Cupeno 1, 9, 4, 46, 67
Cuyamaca 35
Cuyamaca Complex 9-10

-D-

Depletion of Native Grasses . . . 14
Derby Dike 29
Derby, George 22, 29
Diegueno 5, 35, 46
Disease 13, 14, 57, 59
Dryden, D.A. 76, 81-83
Dunn, William B. 19, 20
Dyke, George 30

-E-

Eagle 29
Economic Subsistence 36
El Cajon 13
El Corral 13
Emory, William H. 15-16
Encinitas Tradition 7
Encomienda 15, 33
Ensico 27
Ensworth, Augustus S. 30
Estudillo, Francisco 80, 83
Exclusionary Acts 44

-F-

Fernandez, Ferdinand 39
Fillmore, Millard 1
Fort Leavenworth 19
Foster, Joseph 30
Franciscan 13
Francisco (Luiseno Leader) 56
Francisco (2 murdered Indian) . 26
Frontier Mentality 18
Fugitive Slave Laws 41

-G-

Gara, Antonio 46,47
Gifford, E.B. 23
Gold Rush 18
Goodrich, Chauncey S. 44
Grant's Peace Policy . . . 63, 65-66,
                          69, 74, 84, 88
Grant, Ulysess S 1, 63, 65, 69,
                              73-75, 84
Greene, Augustus P. 22, 65-69
Guatay 35

-H-

Haraszthy, Agoston 46
Harris Site 7
Hatam, Manuel 49
Hawaii (Sandwich Islands) 29
Hayes, Benjamin . . . 33, 48, 50, 52,
                              67-68, 71
Hayes, Rutherford B. 89
Helm, Chatham 25-26
Helm, Turner 23
Henley, Thomas J. 51-53, 60
Highland Valley 65
Horton, Alonzo 76
Hot Springs 26
Hotchkiss, Albert B. 76
Hunsacker, Nicholas 76, 78

Hurtado, Albert 29

-I-

Inaja Reservation 84
Indentured Servitude ...32, 38, 42
Indian Agents 48, 50, 52, 56,
                            72, 88
Indian Burials 28
Indian Children 31-32, 38-39
Indian Education 44
Indian Flogging 42, 50
Indian Fund (California) 38
Indian Fund (San Diego)......28
Indian Labor 31-32, 38, 41-42
Indian Leadership 50-52, 56,
                      66-72, 84, 86
Indian Population...........34
Indian Resistance/
  "Uprisings," 56, 82
Indian Reservations,
  (refer to specific name)
  ....60, 74, 76, 84, 86, 88
Indian Taxation 46
Indian Testimony............22
Indigent Indians 28
Ipai...........1, 4, 9, 57, 60-61

-J-

Jacumba 89
Jamacha 35
Jamul Valley 23
Jacksonian Democracy........39
Jackson, Helen H. 26, 41, 89
Jeffersonian Democracy.......39
Johnson, Andrew 63
Johnston, Adam 45, 60, 63
Jase (Indian tracker) 28-29
Jose......................23

Jose Antonio.........70, 72, 91
Julian 25

-K-

Kearny, Stephan Watts 19, 47
Keller, Don Mateo...........83
Kemble, E.C. 83
Kumeyaay.................4, 9

-L-

La Cronica 76
Laguna Mountains 5
Lagoon Siltation 8
La Jolla (band) 51
La Jolla Complex 6, 8
La Jolla Culture I, II, III.......7
La Jolla (rancheria) .35, 57, 64, 67
Lake Wohlford..............65
La-pinchi 67
La Puerta 67
La Puerta de la Cruz 57, 61
Lea, Luke 46
Leonard, Joseph 32
Lincoln, Abraham 2, 54
Liquor Trade....21-23, 27, 29, 31,
                  38, 41-42, 57, 72
Locke......................71
Lorenzo 35
LA 67, 79, 83, 84
Los Angeles County 27
Los Angeles Express 79, 81-82
Los Angeles Star, ...48, 60, 83
Los Coyotes 35
Lovett, W.E. 51, 56-58, 66
Luiseno ...1, 4-5, 9, 29-30, 34-35,
46, 53, 57-58, 60, 61, 66-71, 86-87, 91

-M-

Machado, Jesus 21

Marone .23
Marron, Don Juan Maria 21
Mataguay 35
Maxcy, Mrs. 32
Medithermal Period 6
Mesa Chiquita 35
Mesa Grande 29-30, 35
Mesa Grande Indians 50, 54
Meti .30
Mexican Land System 14-16
Mexican Period 14
Mexican Ranchos 16
Mexican War 59
McCain Massacre 89
McCorkle, Joseph W. 47
McKee, Redick 45, 47
Milling Horizon (Early) 6-8
Milling Horizon (Late) 6, 9-10
Mission Bay 13
Mission Indians 4, 60
Mission San Diego de Alcala30, 35
Mission San Luis Rey . .19, 57, 69
Modoc Lava Beds 80
Modoc War 73, 80
Mojave Desert 5
Mono Lake. 5
Moreno, Don Jose Jesus 21
Moriarty, James R. 8
Morse, Ephraim 31, 32, 56
Mount Woodson 65
Murietta (rancher) 78-79

-N-

National Republican 76
Neti 30
Noyes, W.H. 28, 32

-O-

Oglesby 73
Old Town 28-29

Olegario . .66-73, 75, 78-84, 85, 91

-P-

Pablo, Pedro 73
Pala . .35, 57, 63-65, 67, 69, 73, 81
                          84, 86-88, 91
Pala Mountain. 65
Pala Reservation 64, 66, 84
Paleo-Indians 6
Palomar Mountain 65
Panto (Mesa Grande) . . .51, 53-54,
                                72, 91
Parker, E.S. 65, 68
Pascoe, James 78
Pauma 35, 53, 59
Pauma Complex 7
Pawii .67
Petroglyphs 10
Phillips, George Harwood . . .2-17
Pico, Pio. 20
Pierce, Franklin 1
Pictographs 10
Potrero 35, 53, 57, 67, 84
Potrero Reservation 84
Prehistory. 5
Presidio Hill. 28
Prostitution 21, 29
Puerto Chiquita 35, 57, 67
Puerto de la Cruz 35, 67
Pujol (rancher) 78
Purdy, Samuel 47

-Q-

Quakers 65

-R-

Ramona 31
Rancho Bernardo 53
Rancho Buena Vista 20

Rancho Cuca 84, 86
Rancho Santa Fe 7
Rapes 13, 19, 21
Rice Canyon 65
Rincon 13, 35, 78
Rock art 5, 9
Rogers, Malcolm 5, 7
Romero, Pedro 22
Rosaria 22
Rosekrans, Mr. 32
Rose, Louis 71
Royce, Josiah 37

-S-

Saboba 35, 57
Sacramento Record Union . . 82-83
San Bernardino 65
San Bernardino Tribes 56
San Bernardo 53
San Diego County Board of
    Supervisors 28
San Diego County
    Taxation on Indians 46
    Indian Indigent Policy . . . 27-29
San Diego Grand Jury 27
San Diego Herald . . 19, 22-23, 29,
                              51, 53
San Diego Reservations 85
San Diego River 29
San Diego Union . . 36, 22, 26, 28,
    66-67, 70, 75-76, 79-81, 83, 86
San Dieguito 35
San Dieguito Complex 6
San Dieguito I, II, III
    Culture 5, 7
San Dieguito Tool Types 7
San Francisco Alta . . 58, 66, 79-80
San Francisco Bulletin 80
San Felipe 15, 35
San Jose de Valle 35
San Luis Rey . . . 35, 50, 64, 86, 88

San Luis Rey Complex 10
San Luis Rey River 7, 9
San Pasqual . . 21-22, 26-27, 30, 64
                              88, 91
San Pasqual Reservation . . 64, 66,
                              68, 70
Santa Rosa 57
San Timoteo 57-58
Santa Ysabel 15, 35, 89
Santa Ysabel Reservation 84
San Ysidro 35, 57, 67
Sarah McFarland 29
Saujarjo (rancher) 78
Seed Gathering Economy 8
Sexton, M.M. 28
Schiller, Marcus 71
Scraper Maker Culture 5
Segregation of Indian Burials . . 28
Sequan 84
Sequan Reservation 84
Shellfish Exploitation 8
Shell Midden People 7
Shoshonean Language 9
Shoshonean Peoples 8
Smith, Edward P. 72, 73, 76
Smith, John P. 84, 88
Smith, Joseph 32
Snook, Mrs. Francisco 22
Sole 23, 25
Soledad 19
Sorrento Valley 19
Spaniards 9, 13-14
Spring Valley 23
Stand Watie 1
Stanley, John, Q.A. 57, 61, 63
Statute 133 . . . (see An Act for the
        Government and Protection
                      of Indians)
Stockton, T.C. 86
Stuart, A.H.H. 45
Subria, Felipe 20
Subria, Maria la Gradia 20

Sumner, Charles 70

-T-

Taggart, Charles P......66, 69, 76
Taylor, N.G. 61, 63, 65
Tejon Indians...............50
Tejon Reservation 50, 52
Temecula 35, 46, 53, 57, 67,
                        78-79, 83
Thompson, John.............70
Tipai 1, 4, 9, 57, 61, 89
Tomas (San Pasqual) ...29, 50-52
Treaty Commissioners 46
Treaty of Guadalupe Hidalgo ..14
                        16, 18, 59, 72
True, Delbert L..............10
Truijillo, Margarita 84
Tule Indians 50
Tyson, J.W. 76

-U-

Ubach 71
United States Senate 47, 48

-V-

Valle de los Viejos...........35
Vallecitos 15, 35, 67
Varela, Antonio 84
Vigilantes 23, 25-26

-W-

Warner Hot Springs 25, 89
Warner, John J. 15
Warner's Ranch 15
Wentworth, John P.H. 54
Wetmore, Charles ...15-16, 30, 33,
                        73, 75-76, 78
Whiting, B.C.......58, 61, 63, 69,

Wilson, Benjamin D. ...29, 48, 50
Wilson, Christopher N. .73, 79-80
Wiley, Austin 57
Wilmington Journal 56
Wolfskill, John 30
Woods, William..............25
Worcester v. Georgia.........39
Wozencraft, Oliver M.45-48, 52, 54

-Y-

Yapitchah 35
Yuman language 9
Yuman Peoples 8